DOWN

ON THE FARM

Dear Bonnie,
Hope you
enjoy the book.
Karen

DOWN

ON THE FARM

Karen T. Dauer

Forward by David E. Klimek, Ph.D.

WINSTED PUBLICATIONS * ANN ARBOR

DOWN ON THE FARM

Cover design by Chris Klimek

Library of Congress Catalog Card Number: 93-060298

ISBN: 0-9630213-2-X

Manufactured in the United State of America.

The Christian is like the ripening corn;
the riper he grows,
the more lowly he bends his head.

~ ~ Thomas Guthrie

Above all else, guard your heart
for it is the wellspring of life.

~ ~ Proverbs 4:23

DEDICATION

I dedicate this book to my husband, Fred. Without his loving encouragement and understanding I would never have had the strength to remember the past.

To my children, Jeffrey, Bill, Kenneth, Miles, Mary, and Mitch, who have all been supportive and helpful in recalling the forgotten pieces of my life, I also dedicate this book with love.

CONTENTS

FORWARD

I feel honored to write a forward for this book. One reason it is easy for me to endorse this work is that it doesn't fit into neat, politically correct or socially convenient categories, hence it tends to unpretentiously parallel life and the many surprises it has in store for each of us. Ms. Dauer's astute insights, and at times her brutal self-honesty, will make all of us feel a little uncomfortable. For as we take time to be quiet and reflect upon ourselves and some of our deepest feelings, we see that Ms. Dauer has candidly articulated many of these struggles. This was not intended to be a women's book per se, but I suspect many women will be able to easily identify with some of the threat, upheaval, change, loss, catastrophe, and psychological and spiritual victories captured in this inspirational volume. Ms. Dauer's literary and poetic style add a freshness that will touch and stimulate the tender places in the heart of the reader.

Often in our fantasies, when life is coming at us a little too fast and the responsibilities seem overwhelming, we imagine how wonderful it would be if we could escape from the frantic pace to a safe haven or to a moment in time when life seemed simpler. Perhaps we imagine ourselves in a pastoral rural setting with an abundance of open space, lush forests, clean rivers and lakes, blue skies, singing birds, radiant sunshine, and vividly colored wildflowers. In our fantasies many of us take ourselves to the uncomplicated, rural, Norman Rockwell settings; to a time when neighbors knew each other, children were carefree, living was simple, and people were honest, trustworthy, loving, and friendly. The manuscript for Down on the Farm was written with just such an idyllic backdrop. Ms. Dauer has lived in rural Minnesota for 53 years. This is a part of America where there are large family farms, thousands of acres of rich farm land, and quaint white frame or antique brick churches with their steeples rising conspicuously toward the heavens. The setting for this volume could be any rural area, anywhere in the world, where generations of hard working families worked the sometimes unforgiving land with their sons and daughters and grandchildren.

Yet, despite this idyllic external environment, psychologically and spiritually, Ms. Dauer brings out the commonality of the human condition, a similarity of living within the hearts of men and women wherever they might choose to reside. Beneath the exteriors of even the most idyllic circumstances, humans confront similar problems related to earning a living, raising children, and trying to remain enthusiastically in love while adjusting to relatives, community, and extended family. Each of us must also come to grips with our own aloneness, interpersonal conflicts, limitations in our personal development, numerous separations, painful losses, disappointments, frustrations, and unrealized dreams, and then make the most out of daily living.

Some of us, and Ms. Dauer is one such person, are dealt some unexpected emotional blows that knock us to our knees, thus paving the way for humility and prayer. She carefully conveys her befuddlement, anger, confusion, and desperation at the tragic death of her husband, and the slow and tedious resolve of her despair to a more integrated, higher level ego state. Regardless of how hard we try to make ourselves feel secure, loved, and happy, all the while trying to remain appreciative of daily living, seldom do we proceed smoothly.

In this descriptive volume, Ms. Dauer articulates with candor some of her personal struggles of trying to raise six children, her feelings of dubious self-worth, her medical difficulties, and the beginnings of her psychological and spiritual awakening. She rather straightforwardly relates her spiritual dilemmas and satisfactions, her feelings of heresy when she began to question her upbringing and religious training, and the tragedy and slow recovery from her husband's abrupt, accidental death. In many respects this book is a fairly detailed description of one woman's courageous efforts to rise above her debilitating self-doubt and feelings of low self-worth, her "old fashioned" and repressive upbringing, to a place where she can now hold her head high.

She proceeds through the pages of this book carefully detailing the discovery of her God-given, yet hidden, reservoir of personal talent, intelligence, and peace of mind that had been unknown to her until she discovered a therapist who helped her realize her potential. As she began to resolve her deep feelings of worthlessness and intellectual stagnation, she fairly quickly actualized her intellectual potential to acquire her Bachelors and Masters degrees.

Throughout this book Ms. Dauer speaks freely of her spiritual faith and some of her Christian convictions that helped her get through those times when she was emotionally and spiritually depleted, and felt as though she might not have the strength or desire to go on. Yet she did go on, and, through honest soul-searching and spiritual faith, was able to overcome many of the obstacles that imprison some people in a lesser quality of living.

Down On The Farm will be inspirational to all women who have gradually lost themselves in the complicated and noble endeavor of trying to be a super-responsible wife, mother, employee, and community and church leader. It will be especially helpful to women who have experienced the most painful loss of all, that of a person who was deeply loved. Whether that person was a husband, lover, parent, friend, or child, re-experiencing the pain through a reflective reading of Ms. Dauer's story will assist in further healing.

David Klimek Ph.D.
The Gardener

PREFACE

This book is a sharing of struggles and the realization that I did not have to search for or find God, for He had already found me and was showing me His love every day. Albert Schweitzer was once asked for the most profound truth he knew, and he replied, "Jesus loves me." Knowing that Jesus still loves me, even when I feel I am unlovable, gives me strength in some of my darkest days.

I believe that God created us each to be unique. I believe that different is divine. My early religious training, however, taught me that different is bad and wrong, that God has a mold and all good people look the same. Through a long process of growth and new understanding, my beliefs have changed significantly. I no longer feel that unity means uniformity. I believe the idea that everyone has to conform has hurt both the quality of our relationships and our ability to be fully productive, fully alive, human beings.

What I want to stress in this book is that we are all free to be unique individuals if we choose to be, and that this freedom is a blessing to be treasured and utilized. When I began to accept that different is not only alright but also good, I became far less competitive. If we are each listening to the message of our own heart, to the inner voice of God, then there's no need to compete against anyone else; we're all winners. If we each do what we're meant to do, and do it to the best of our ability, then there's no need for jealousy, rivalry, or hostility. Each of us will be uncovering and expressing our own individual truth, and then sharing it with others. I do not want to convey the idea that we need to be rebelliously independent. That attitude has hindered many movements, such as the women's movement. To be rebellious gets in the way of finding one's own truth, because the focus is external, fighting against others, rather than internal, listening to and following one's own soul.

Each of us has a special gift given to us by God; one that no one else on earth has been given. Just as we have different hand and foot prints, and even voice prints, so, too, do we each have a singular path to travel; a private journey that can be completed only by the individual. To be jealous of others, to be competitive with others, or to covet what someone else has been given, is to deny our own distinctive talent or path.

There is no isolation if being different is cherished, for then we can honestly believe that one plus one equals more than two. In other words, if I am eager to hear your perspective, then I can add mine to yours and we will come up with more than the sum of our two perspectives. To approach and create experiences in this way adds new dimensions to our relationships and enriches all of life.

When I began, through therapy, to discover my own uniqueness and found it to be good, I recall saying, "The very things I hated most about myself are some of my greatest gifts, and the things I thought were wonderful are really just me trying to act like something I am not." This was a hard lesson to learn, one I still work on daily. The hardest part for me was to quit defending myself and my actions. Once I learned to hear the therapist, which took several months, I began to integrate these new ideas into my value system and apply them to my life. The results have been extremely rewarding, for my life now is richer and more honest.

It's heartening to know that there are people who value authenticity. There appear to be more and more people who are tired of the fluff, the flesh, and the flash so prevalent in America today. When one travels beyond our shores and has a chance to view our country a little more objectively, it's embarrassing to see some of the things we stand for as a nation, and what we choose to show to the rest of the world. It is reassuring to see that we appear to be approaching the time when more and more people want something that is authentic; that more people are seeking truth.

Lest the reader think this is just another book about positive thinking and pulling one's self up by the boot straps, let me emphasize that I could not have grown, could not have accepted the truth, without God. Throughout my life I have been aware of God's presence in my life. He has always been a very real help to me. In some of the most difficult circumstances, even if I could not feel His presence, I would still press on with the confidence that He would guide me, possibly in ways I could not comprehend. I did not always feel His presence, especially after the death of my husband, yet in retrospect, surely He directed me to the place I am now.

Summer 1993
Karen Thormodson-Dauer

CHAPTER 1

DANDELION DAYS

We shall not cease from exploration and the end of all our exploring will be to arrive where we started and know the place for the first time.

~ ~ T. S. Eliot

He who does the duty of his own nature incurs no sin.

~ ~ Srimad-Bhagawad-Gita

THE ROSE

I am a flower. My name is Rose. I've always been a rose, only I didn't know it. Now I do. Today I do. For many years I was told to be a dandelion, and I really tried. I changed my colors so I looked almost yellow, except in rare moments of truth. I was careful not to be too real, too rose. I stayed where other dandelions grew. Lots of them; the more the better. But it was important that I be the biggest and brightest. Occasionally another dandelion might notice my pink fringe, but I pretended not to notice. I felt bad because I didn't look exactly right. I tried so hard to fit in.

Then one day I met a gardener. He walked slowly through the garden and it was almost as though he could see beneath the yellow, could even see the rose.

I was astounded. How dare he? What if he were to expose me to the other dandelions? What would I do? I'd never be able to face them again. For weeks I worried about them finding out. I was sure not many, if any, ever suspected my true color and shape. Oh, what if he told them, and how did he know?

I tried to look like the other dandelions. I nodded my head with each breeze. I'm sure it was right. I looked exactly the way I thought he wanted a good dandelion to look. I even tried to catch the dewdrops on my petals and shine all the time. But somehow he always saw the rose beneath the glitter. I tried so hard. Didn't he know dandelions were preferred? I thought everyone knew that. Why did he insist I be a rose? I was angry. See how many dandelions there are? If God had wanted me to be a rose, surely he wouldn't have made me look like a dandelion!

Then I began to see. God made me like He wanted me. He really needed and wanted and loved me as a rose. I was the one who changed. Somehow my mom and dad had been taught that dandelions were better. Everyone in my family had been a dandelion. I came from a long, strong line. Many of my relatives and friends were dandelions who didn't seem to like roses very much. Why would I decide to be a rose? It was just not proper. Everyone knew that.

Regularly and steadily The Gardener came. I feel the dewdrops on my petals still as I recall the gentle compassion mixed with twinges of sadness in his eyes. It was alright with him if I chose to remain a dandelion, or tulip, or thistle, or violet. For he loved all flowers and the word "weed" was not in his vocabulary. I knew that. Many times I tried to get him to call me a weed, treat me like a weed, and just pull me from the garden. Other times I would angrily display my ugliness, hoping to convince him of my lowly status. But he steadfastly refused to play my game.

I couldn't see then that my roots were those of a rose. All my life, in a very small part of my stem and leaves and roots and center, I had always been a rose. No matter how I tried to change the shape, height, and color, my essence remained true to its origins.

For a long time I blamed God and others; I especially blamed The Gardener, as he gently nurtured and hoed and cultivated. His gentleness, however, finally got to me. The soft touch of his pruning and fertilizing never hurt for too long, but the cultivator blade sometimes went deep. As my leaves healed I saw different contours take shape, from sharp and pointed to rounded edges. My leaves no longer poked or hurt other dandelions. That was the first change. Then my roots deepened and my stem started to grow and strengthen and I could see farther than ever before. I even saw a few roses. Maybe it wasn't so bad to be a rose. There were several roses and no one appeared to be chopping them down.

The roses...how beautiful! I saw them standing straight and tall, blossoming freely and just letting all the other flowers alone. They never once told the dandelions to be roses, or the violets to grow taller, or the lily of the valley to grow in the sun instead of the shade. They didn't even explain how much better off the dandelions would be if they moved from the north side of the house to the south side. But I noticed something else. All the time I had been a dandelion, I kept hassling the other dandelions. I was always telling them how to grow, how to be, and mostly how uncomfortable they made me. Why didn't they just be like me with pink around the edges and we'd all get along better? Now, with my softer, rounded contours, I noticed that I, too, no longer poked or hurt the other dandelions. I just let them live.

Still, The Gardener came once a week. And still God sent His wind and rain and sunlight. I no longer hated God for the emerging rose. I no longer rebelled against my parents for my dandelion characteristics, for they had not experienced many roses, only glimpses now and then. Often they were so involved with themselves, they who were beginning to change from yellow to flimsy white, they hadn't been too concerned about me or my color. And I, with my own self-focus, had only seen them as bright yellow and young, the way I remembered them, the way they'd always been. Now I looked again and saw the soft seeds and fluffy white and was amazed. Sometimes we all have difficulty seeing others clearly.

Then it hit me. Only God, The Gardener, and I had ever seen the real rose. For me, it had been so long ago and I'd tried very hard to forget. For God, He loved both roses and dandelions, but had chosen to make me a rose. So in the right season God sent a gardener to encourage the rose, and to help remove the many damaged, withered, and superfluous petals and nurture the few, but precious, real ones.

Today I am a rose. Sometimes I still need The Gardener, but more often I just enjoy watching him walk through the Garden of the Living and smile. He looks at all Life and sees it for what it is, always appreciating the uniqueness of all living things and their different stages of development. Whether in bud or bloom or dormant, he knows it is genuine and he smiles.

God still sends His wind and rain and sunshine. His visits seem more comfortable now. No longer does He seem cruel for making me a rose. Here I stand. I am a rose. I have a right to be here. No more or less than any of God's creatures. My one regret is that I waited so long to unsheathe my truth.

* * * * * * * *

I was reluctant to use this piece. It reveals so much of the therapy process and, because of that, still hurts a little. But I believe that the message contained in <u>The Rose</u> is an important one. We all have a rose within, but often it is found only through a painful process. For myself, I could not have revealed my blossom without help. I am convinced that in order to find ourselves we often need another person. We most assuredly do not need groups or crowds if our only motive is to try to use others to support our facades and our illusions.

Groups can be helpful later, when there is a real self to reinforce, but not when we are just beginning the process.

The one I found who helped me find my truth and my rose was a therapist, the one I refer to as The Gardener. That was the beginning. However, even once the truth is glimpsed it does not automatically follow that the rose will be brought forth. That The Gardener could see the inner person, the person beneath all my pretense, did nothing for me except make me feel exposed, threatened, and angry. I had to discover the truth about myself, by myself, over many months and even years, of painful awakenings.

The place where each of us needs to begin the process of transformation is with the family of origin. No matter what life brings today, it has been built on yesterday; the first few years of life set the tone, the patterns, and the way we feel about the self. Until I could go back and experience the pain and rejection, the destructive attitudes and beliefs I felt from those early years, I could not begin to heal the hurt nor allow my true self to emerge.

As I embarked on my therapeutic journey, I began to see that my outward bragging and facade of well-being covered a bankrupt interior. I repeatedly said how great I was, yet I felt like I was the worst person on earth. I genuinely believed that God had somehow made a mistake when He created me. My misery had to do in part with my trying so hard to follow the rules set down by others, especially the church. I did my best to follow the rules, yet I was miserable; therefore I must be the problem, I must be the sinner among sinners. Everyone else seemed perfectly happy and content, without problems and without sin.

While trying to make sense out of my belief that everyone else was good and happy, and that I was defective and miserable, I was haunted by the words of a speech I gave in high school. I was 18 years old, and the speech was built around the following:

> And the high man takes the high way
> And the low man takes the low
> And in-between on the misty flats
> The rest drift to and fro
> But for everyone there openeth
> A high way and a low
> And everyone decideth the way his
>   Soul shall go.
>
> ~ ~ Unknown

Perhaps, I realized, other people only <u>seem</u> happy and content and in reality they are "on the misty flats drifting to and fro." I now realize too, with some sadness, that most people do not even know there is any way to live other than the way they have always lived. They have fallen into patterns and never question their existence. Their lives, as Thoreau stated, are lives of "quiet desperation;" they may be busy but they are barren.

Through therapy I began to learn another way of life, a way of peace and contentment. I also learned that one of the ways of finding inner peace is to trust the process of living and just let Life unfold. If I were to tell you the path I have trod it would seem anything but orthodox, certainly not straight. There are things I am ashamed of and some I would do differently. Yet when I look back, all of the pieces of my life brought me to where I am today and were necessary in their own ways.

Years later, while working on my master's degree, I attended a seminar on how children form their early view of God based on interactions with those in their immediate environment. As a youngster I saw God as punitive, distant, and cold, probably even vengeful. Unfortunately, we carry these beliefs with us throughout life and they have a profound effect on how we view ourselves and others. It was only in the process of therapy that I began to develop a different perception of what genuine love and caring can be, and I thereby gained a new spiritual awareness and connection with God.

There is a special gratitude in my heart to The Gardener for coming into my life and helping me find myself. I used to talk about my search for "me." Well, I have been found...and I like myself. I still don't fit into the mainstream, but I no longer need to. I live a very private life. I follow my own path. Sometimes I go where there are crowds, but not often. The pathological drive to perform is gone, and I no longer feel the need to please everyone. (During my dandelion days particularly, I felt obligated to please everyone.) In becoming all things to all people, it is possible to become nothing to anyone.

It was with The Gardener's help that I began to see how important it is, first and foremost, that I please myself, for, in the end, it will be I who will find either fulfillment or misery at the conclusion of this earthly life. I have learned to live my life the way I want to and, just as importantly, to let others live life their way.

Mostly now I try just to enjoy each moment of life. I have the inner voice of The Gardener and my new spiritual awareness to help me in my daily decision-making process. I think, "What would I be doing if I were doing what's best for me...?" In asking myself this question I'm learning to love myself as well as others.

A friend of mine who grows roses commercially says he learned a lot about life and love, not through therapy, but by tending his flowers. He shared with me that when he first started growing roses he desperately tried to do it "right." He gave his roses everything he felt they wanted or needed. He followed the manufacturer's directions to the letter, but not all plants flourished. Many dried up and died.

He went on to say:

> "At first they produced abundantly, but then, almost imperceptibly, they began to show signs of weakness and, with the first test of stress, they were unable to survive. I learned that giving with reckless abandon is not the answer. I started listening to the plants and using my own good judgment. To make them strong, I'd occasionally put obstacles in their paths, such as temporarily withholding food or water. I made sure they had adequate amounts of sunlight *and* darkness, for the darkness is equally important. I learned that plants are a lot like people. There is a rhythm to it all, and my part was to find the pulse of the individual plants. I have spent my life trying to find the perfect balance."

It is also interesting that two brothers ran this greenhouse. One loved the roses, the other was just doing a job. There was a visible difference between the products that emerged. The roses grown with love, respect, and care were bigger, brighter, and lasted almost twice as long in the homes of customers as the roses grown in a halfhearted, mechanistic manner. I, too, learned a lot about love from my friend and his vibrant roses.

Each plant is different and has its own likes and dislikes. However, just as we, too, have things we prefer over others, it seems with both plants and people, balance is the magic quality. For plants it is the balance between light, temperature, water, and nutrition. With people it seems to be necessary to have not only balanced meals for physical well-being, but the proper balance of emotional and spiritual nourishment as well.

Today the way I keep the rose blooming is through total awareness in the present, which is made possible only by honestly looking at the past, no matter how difficult that may be. I believe when Jesus said "Narrow is the way and few there are who find it," He meant the easy way of living is one of just coasting along with the crowd, filling up time and space, oblivious to our own deepest nature. To question ourselves and really get to know ourselves is the narrow way. It takes time, energy, and tears...and it is a painfully lonely journey. Most people believe it is not worth the effort.

In the following pages I hope to show that it is worth the effort. When I was alone on the farm all day with six children, it would have been reassuring to have known that everyone struggles with life; that no one has all the answers; and that, with work and will, we can overcome our inner struggles and live a richer life filled with satisfaction. It seems that our greatest obstacle is the inherent resistance to change. We are such complicated creatures and we try very hard to defend our actions and protect our vulnerabilities. We need many tools to help us release our inner rose: a strong support system to sustain us and accept us, even with all our thorns and inconsistencies. Depending upon the damage we have incurred during our early years, we may or may not need a professional therapist to help us become honest with who we really are at any given moment. We also need an arsenal of strength and a great deal of determination to face ourselves. With these tools, the process of self-discovery and individuation becomes merely challenging rather than insurmountable...and the payoff is a profound and exciting new view of Life.

NO PLACE TO BE SAD

Thank you for being sad with me today.
In this world of always having to smile and pretend
It was so nice to just have a space to mend,
To let my mask fall to the ground
And expose my soul with no one around
Except you and your gentle looks.
Thank you for not just giving me a book
I don't have the strength to read right now;
Too many issues on this fevered brow.
So few places to let my tears show,
Maybe that's why I'm always on the go.
Where does one go when their world falls apart?
Where can one cry and make a fresh start?
In this world of doing and spending
Where do I find space to start my life's mending.
I'm not talking of sewing or mending nets.
I'm talking of feelings and minds that are set.
Like clocks in our brain they tick, tick away
With all of the messages of what other's say.
What I need is a space to not have to hurry,
A place that is safe with no need to worry.
I know what I need, for I've been that space
For several others in this hurting old race.
Now I need someone to be that for me;
A place where the "I" of me can become "we."

If but for an hour you'll give me your time
And hear what I say between the lines,
I'll tell you my story, and I guess we both know
That is how our hurting Soul's grow.

CHAPTER 2

SUNLIGHT AND SHADOWS:

THOUGHTS AND INSIGHTS FROM LIFE

Blessed is the man who finds wisdom, the man who gains understanding, for she is more profitable than silver, and yields better returns than gold.

~ ~ Proverbs 3:13-14

The unexamined life is not worth living.

~ ~ Plato

Self-discovery is attained only by travelling a long, rough, twisted path. The discoveries along the way are sometimes beautiful revelations, seeming suddenly to weave together all the dangling threads of life into a brilliant and elegant whole. Other discoveries are brutal and horrid; they rip open your heart, your mind, and your soul; they brand you with Truth, and leave your once cherished beliefs lying scattered in ashes.

During the time I was in therapy, and for years after, as I began looking at myself and at the world with new eyes, I kept journals. Sometimes I wrote at length, but often I just quickly jotted down my latest insight, knowing full well that no attempt to express it in words could ever truly capture the movement that had taken place in my heart.

What follows are a few of those insights, as well as thoughts and insights that I value which were picked up along Life's way; insights which I have heard repeated in various forms, with different words, but with the same undertones, by others who have also been on the inward journey to wholeness.

* * * * * *

In any given situation, I come in with so many attitudes already in place, it's hard to give myself or others a fair chance. Usually I've already decided for you how you will react and what you are feeling without asking, so I've been judge and jury within three minutes after we've met.

* * * * * *

I'm very accepting when I feel acceptable, and I'm just as rejecting when I feel rejected.

* * * * * *

I let everyone determine everything I feel, except me.

* * * * * *

If I feel ill at ease with you, the problem is with me.

* * * * * *

I hate you for messing up my expectations with your reactions. But I get angry with myself for not knowing better how you would respond.

* * * * * *

I have a hundred ways to make myself lose - and I enlist your help.

* * * * * *

I let people dump on me so I can feel justifiably hurt.

* * * * * *

I am amazed at the lengths to which I am willing to go to either receive or avoid pain, depending on which is needed.

* * * * * *

How often as a child I pretended to be asleep. How often as an adult I pretend to be awake!

* * * * * *

Juvenile delinquents come in all ages. Rebellion is part of the human condition.

* * * * * *

If somebody risks something different than I do, I don't recognize it as risk.

* * * * * *

I'm so afraid of me, I have trouble seeing you.

* * * * * *

Like water, I seek people of my own depth.

* * * * * *

Forgive those who misuse your friendship by realizing how their own special problems and bruises hinder them.

* * * * * *

My father gave me wonderful words of advice that come back to me often. Three of these gems of wisdom that have proven true:

"Don't ever loan money, especially to relatives. It will ruin the relationship. Give it to them. If they pay it back, that's a bonus."

"One will never get rich farming, but it is the best place to raise children."

"Even if there were not a heaven or hell, I would still pattern my life after the Bible, for it is the best way to live."

* * * * * *

The Lord knows the needs of each heart and draws together those who have similar needs or modes of expression, that we may comfort each other in our sorrows and share with each other our joys.

* * * * * *

There will always be "one more thing to do." I will never get all caught up. Yet time is equally given to everyone, and I can decide to be driven or to be the driver.

* * * * * *

To a mind that is still, the whole universe surrenders.

* * * * * *

I like feeling that I am happening to life instead of it just happening to me, or in spite of me. Having said that, I'm aware of how easy are these words and how difficult is this action.

* * * * * *

Farming is faith in action. Every day presents a new challenge. It takes almost more courage than I sometimes have to trust in God rather than in a regular pay check.

* * * * * *

What you perceive as outside yourself trying to get in, is really inside trying to get out; like a dark pit craving sunlight. When you allow your darkness expression, then the light comes pouring in.

* * * * * *

It is a sobering discovery to realize, to comprehend, that people will be little changed, little moved, little affected by what you say. But look out for what you are! That's how it is in communication - you, your heart, are being heard, not your words. Your words of love are believed when they are seen in action, when they are experienced first hand, not when stated as fact. Love is received when it is felt, not when it is spoken in syllables.

* * * * * *

The gift of making friends is one of life's greatest gifts.

* * * * * *

All motivation, on some level, is selfish.

* * * * * *

I cannot control what hurts me but I can control how I respond to that hurt.

* * * * * *

Life is a series of choices. Through my priorities I decide what my legacy will be.

* * * * * *

The amount of resistance to growth is in direct proportion to the hopes and dreams I have. Little goals present slight resistance. Bigger goals present quite a challenge.

* * * * * *

Many people live, really live, only one year and then they repeat that year 20 times, again and again. My goal is to live each experience only once and to experience as much as possible in my life.

* * * * * *

There are at least six ways to do anything. My way of getting something done is not right and yours wrong; they are just different, and different is okay.

* * * * * *

Creating time for one's dreams and goals will always be a challenge.

* * * * * *

I cannot be all things to all people without losing myself.

* * * * * *

There is no limit to the good I can do if I can forget about who gets the credit.

* * * * * *

If you imagine that I love you for you, you are fooling yourself. I love you for me. For in loving you I love me. In my ability to love another, I like myself better; I can accept and not reject myself. Thus, I can accept and love you.

* * * * * *

This last insight about loving was a long time in coming. It was about ten years after my therapist helped me to see that all motivation is selfish; it is always for self-interest or self-preservation. I had tried very hard to prove that wrong in my life. I wanted to believe I loved others simply for who they were; that they needed my love and I really didn't need theirs. I wanted to believe my motives were purely altruistic.

Then one night a friend was telling me how unlovable he felt and how grateful he was that I loved him. He acted like I was doing him a big favor by loving him and that made me a wonderful person. I just blurted out, "If you think I love you for you, you're fooling yourself. Don't you realize that in loving you, I love myself? When I focus not just on me and what I want, when I go outside myself and really care about you, then miraculously I accept and love myself more."

It's the same with happiness. When I look for happiness and complain about how unhappy I am and expect someone else to make me happy, I invariably end up miserable. Yet when I forget about myself and just enjoy helping another, I find I am truly happy. Jesus said it better than I when He said, "You reap what you sow."

CHAPTER 3

EVERY LIMB BECOMES STRONGER WHERE ONCE IT WAS BROKEN

Consider it pure joy, my brothers, whenever you face trials of many kinds, because you know that the testing of your faith develops perseverance. Perseverance must finish its work so that you may be mature and complete, not lacking anything. If any of you lacks wisdom, he should ask God, who gives generously to all without finding fault, and it will be given to him.

~ ~James 1:2-5

When I was young, I helped my dad plant a row of trees. The first tree in the row was especially fortunate because it was close enough to the house that we could water it with the hose. The rest were kind of on their own, and the last tree in the row had a special challenge. As it grew, we realized it was too close to the incinerator where we burned the trash. Its leaves were often singed and we gave up on it and expected it to die.

A few weeks ago I was visiting my brother at the old home place, and we were walking through the grove. I came upon the trees and saw that one of them was several feet taller than the others and almost twice as big around. To my amazement, the tree that had lived with adversity was far ahead of the others by any measurement. The pampered one, closest to the house, had blown over years ago, my brother told me, because its roots hadn't gone very deep. With the first big storm it toppled over. The one that had endured hardships had not only survived, but thrived.

In retrospect, now that I can make sense of what has happened, I am glad I endured the hardships in my life. I believe they left me with a much greater understanding of and empathy for others. I have known people with protected childhoods who have had very limited capacity for empathy. My first husband had a very sheltered childhood and didn't have to face any adversity, so it was very hard for him to identify with my struggles. It is only as we are challenged, sometimes to a near breaking point, that we grow.

* * * * *

I was born the fourth child in four years to a mother who taught country school before marrying at 32. My father waited seven years after deciding to marry her before she agreed to marry him. He was 35 at the time. Within four years they were the parents of two boys and two girls. I was the youngest. Within a few months of my birth my mother had a miscarriage.

During my early years I had several medical problems that brought pain, fear, and a terrifying sense of isolation. When I was five years old I began hemorrhaging and it was discovered that the walls of the capillaries of my legs were too thin, and I needed blood transfusions. Then, at six, I needed surgery on my neck to prevent becoming crippled.

It was in a routine visit to a chiropractor with my parents that Dr. Baker told us one cord in my neck was shorter than the other and, without surgery, eventually my whole right side would be deformed and I'd be unable to walk. He explained he could do nothing for me, but at the Mayo Clinic in Rochester they were beginning to do a new type of surgery that could possibly help me. The year was 1946.

My neck problem had given me no pain but, in looking back, even in a photograph of me at three months of age, it is noticeable that I held my head to the right side. So eventually there would have been a muscle imbalance with all the difficulties that presents, pain often being one of them. My eyes, too, would have been affected if nothing were done to correct this.

At that age I knew nothing of what the word "surgery" meant. I knew only that I got to go to someplace called Rochester and I always loved going to new places. My mother began to cry when she got the letter setting up the Mayo Clinic appointment, and I felt confused by that. If this was a good thing we were doing, why cry? If it wasn't a good thing, why do it? I'm sure she was afraid I'd be crippled or would die. I'm also sure they didn't have the money for expensive visits with specialists, nor for surgery.

On my first visit to the clinic I had a thorough check-up. That was fun. I met a lot of doctors and other staff, many of whom gave me candy and gum, and all of whom gave me a lot of attention. I was not used to either of these. Also, my parents and I got to eat at restaurants, which was always a special treat. Best of all I got to be the only child for a brief time, for my brothers and sister had to stay home with my grandparents.

On the return visit, the day before the surgery, I was put into a room and my parents left. Very little had been explained to me, I was anxious about what was going to happen to me, and I didn't understand the fear in my parents' eyes when they left. So there I was, alone for the first time in my young life, not knowing what was to become of me. I thought my parents were leaving me there to die, frightened and alone. I cried but no one heard or cared. The nurse finally came and told me they'd be back for me in the morning. That seemed like forever and, yet, I wasn't so sure I wanted morning ever to arrive.

The room was pale green - the sickly, institutional green of the 1940's - and they were in the process of painting the hall, so my room was filled with paint fumes. Because I was nauseated after the surgery due to the ether, I now associate that color green and the awful smell of paint with nausea and the fear of dying.

Finally morning came. I wasn't allowed to have any breakfast, probably because I'd get even sicker after the surgery if I did, but I didn't understand that and it wasn't explained to me. I was put on a cold, hard, metal table with wheels. My last glimpse of my parents was of my mom crying and my dad trying to comfort her. I didn't understand their fear and it didn't feel good. I knew only that they left me, strapped down and being wheeled away. I was taken down the hall to a cold, intensely lit room. Someone told me to count out loud and the next thing I knew I was back in the hospital room, sick and wanting to vomit, and with a heavy thing all around me which turned out to be the cast. I couldn't even sit up to vomit without a nurse to help me.

The cast was made of plaster of Paris, lined with gauze. Only the top of my head, my face, and my ears were exposed. Otherwise, it completely encased me down to my waist; it was like a vest except it extended up to the top of my head. It kept my neck perfectly still for three months. In six weeks we returned for a check-up and they cut a little window in the cast, looked at the incision, then taped it back up for another six weeks. I remember exactly how I looked; very odd and very unfamiliar - like a freak. My dad often remarked they should have taken a picture, but I would have hated that.

Everywhere I went in public, people looked at me and whispered. I was sure they had never seen such a strange sight. The stares and whispers left me feeling subhuman and isolated, a feeling that was to stay with me for years. The clinic got permission from my parents to take my picture and I've been told they are still using it at the Mayo Clinic Museum in Rochester. Today, because of all the medical advances, when people have this surgery, they wear only a neck brace for a couple months afterwards.

My parents initially were told I'd be in the hospital for three weeks and would have to learn to walk again. They were surprised when three days after the surgery it was decided I was ready to go home. I'd been on a tour of the hospital the night before and several people had offered me candy. I was still nauseated but I didn't want them to feel bad so I took the candy and tried to eat it. Even that long ago I was denying my own feelings. I was still feeling really sick and probably should have stayed at least a few days longer in the hospital, but I tried to look and act healthier than I was. Whatever the nurses suggested I do, I did it to please them whether I felt up to it or not, a response pattern I continued for decades.

By the time I returned home I was feeling incredibly powerless, I think partially due to the fact that the cast weighed nearly as much as I did. I couldn't do anything to get away from it. When it was hot in the house, my skin would itch inside the cast and there was nothing anyone could do to control it. Just moving freely was no longer possible, and I felt weighted down and trapped.

These two medical experiences, the blood transfusions when I was five and the neck surgery at six, were lonely places in my young life. But in my isolation during those times, I became aware of other people and their problems, particularly some of the other children who were in the hospital at the same time. There was a baby who had swallowed a safety pin, a little boy from Africa whom my mother said was going to die, and another little boy in a wheelchair. I remember thinking about them a lot after I went home and realizing there were many kids a lot worse off than I was.

I learned some valuable lessons from the surgery experience. I learned that frightening or negative experiences can turn out good. Even though the cast was heavy and uncomfortable, and after it was removed I had to do special exercises, my neck did heal and was finally straight. I was, however, very conscious of the scar and felt flawed for years until it faded.

My being hospitalized got me a lot of attention and I knew it. For many years following that I felt as though the only way I could get attention was by being sick, so all during my early school years I was sick quite often. It wasn't until years later, however, when I married, that I stopped using illness to get attention. My husband saw sickness as a weakness, so, from that time on, I never let anyone know how I felt, even when I really was sick.

I started country school that same year, but because of the neck surgery I had to quit and start again the following year. However, it wasn't until decades later in therapy that

I made that connection. Until then, I'd always thought it had been because I was so dumb that I'd had to start over. It's these little misperceptions, the often simple but erroneous conclusions a child makes, that can have such a life-long impact on self-image. My mother, for example, has recently shared with me that she was often afraid I was going to die when I was a child. Her fear, however, must have caused her to feel overwhelmed with me because the message I got was that she *wished I would die* because I was too much work and too expensive; a painful and shattering impression for a child to bear.

In those early years my mother was very strict. She had taught at a country school for 14 years where she was responsible for all eight grades. She had been very young and sometimes had as many as 30 students in her classroom, some bigger than she was, and therefore, she had to be a stern authority figure. That trait also, however, ran in the family. Her mother before her had always been the boss of the family. Regardless of where this trait came from, she expected the same kind of behavior and obedience from her own children as she had in the classroom.

My mother had been taught that the important thing was to get results. I'm sure she had never entertained the notion that one can be loved just for *being*; all of her emphasis was on *doing*. Life became one big score board with God listing the points that would measure our worth. That's why, even as a small child, my self-esteem was tied up with pleasing adults. I never felt loved solely for me, but for what I could do, so I ended up selling my soul to the grade givers of life. I felt good only if I had all A's and I focussed and obsessed on all the B's and how to "correct" them. I worked incessantly for all A's, for "thank you"'s, and for people to like me. Even though I eventually overcame a lot of hardships along the way, each success often just brought more anxiety - anxiety that the next time I'd not be able to attain or do "enough."

I was forever joining contests or being in a competition of some sort. Each success just pushed me into wanting more success because each success created a new standard of excellence that must be met or surpassed the next time around. What happened was that my life soon became analogous to my existence in that cast: hard and rigid on the outside, powerless and hopeless on the inside. Because my inner feelings and my outer expressions were so widely divergent, I nearly died inside while I smiled on the outside, all the while being rewarded for this behavior. Years later I expressed it this way:

You ask how I am,
"I'm fine," I say.
But you really don't want to know, do you?

Outside I'm fine, outside I smile,
While my insides twist and hurt like hell.
But you really don't want to know, do you?

Remembering all this brings to mind a story I read long ago about intrinsic worth versus being used for others' gain. I no longer remember where the story came from, but it goes like this:

> A carpenter and his apprentice were walking together through a large forest. When they came across a beautiful old oak tree, huge and gnarled, the carpenter asked his apprentice, 'Do you know why this tree is so huge, so gnarled, so beautiful and old?' The apprentice looked at his Master and said, 'No...why?'
>
> 'Well,' said the carpenter, 'because it is useless. If it had been useful it would have been cut long ago and made into tables and chairs. Only because it is useless could it grow so beautiful and so tall that you can now sit in its shade and relax.'

During these same early years, my mother went through bouts of severe depression. Her depression affected me mostly in that it made me feel overwhelming responsibility. First of all, I was sure it must be my fault because everything bad that happened felt like it was my fault. Also, I desperately wanted my mother to be happy and continually felt responsible for doing the things that would accomplish that. At age four, for example, I'd get a chair and push it over to the sink and wash the dishes after lunch. The other kids were in school so there was just my mom, my dad, the hired man, and me. Sometimes my dad would dry the dishes and we'd sing songs. I still remember the words of the songs he taught me while we did the dishes, but the predominate memory is the feeling of how good it felt to please my mother.

Sometimes my mother would lie on the bed crying, and that always made me feel terribly sad. Sometimes I'd lie next to her and try to cheer her up by repeating things she had taught me, like the 23rd Psalm or a poem. During those times I felt like I was the mother and I needed to take care of her. I now realize that's a terrible burden for a child to bear. Years later when my own children were small, I remember once crying because a friend had died. I picked up my daughter, who was four at the time, and held her close to me as I cried. She patted my back with her little hand and said, "Mommy, I'll take care of you.

Don't cry." I thought, "No, I should be the one taking care of you."

The first sustained relationship I had that was emotionally fulfilling was when, in the fifth grade, I had a teacher who really liked me and told me I had great potential. It wasn't just with words that she made me feel special. She also let me stay at her home overnight and she shared herself with me by talking about deep and important issues, and I felt truly valued for the first time.

This teacher talked to me and helped me understand my early feelings about wearing a cast, for she had had polio as a child and her one leg was shorter than the other, and she wore special shoes, so she had experienced similar feelings of being "different." She also talked to me about many "adult" issues such as dating and choosing a life mate. She told me about her own marriage and how, at one time, she and her husband were living in different places because of his job. She said that no matter what happened, for her entire life she would love only this one man. When she became pregnant I was one of the first to know, and she trusted me to not tell anyone. She always treated me as an equal, and that had a powerful and positive effect on how I felt about myself. Later she was my instructor in declamation speaking contests. She was a great encourager. Once when, as a freshman, I lost to a senior in a contest, she said, "Some things come only with age." I've never forgotten the wisdom and the comfort of those words.

That relationship lasted throughout high school and beyond. She moved away when I was 14, but we continued to write and see each other occasionally. When I married at nineteen she thought it was a mistake, not because of my choice of a partner, but because she felt that some people have something to offer in life beyond being wives and mothers, and she believed I was one of those people. She had hoped I'd complete college before marriage. "I'm sure you could have a career as well as a family," she said. After more than 35 years, I still remember those words and the look of sadness on her face.

In spite of all her concerns for me, I did marry at 19 and moved on with my life, stronger and wiser for having experienced both adversity and at least one truly kind and loving soul.

TREES

The trees are bare.
Does anyone care
That the trees are bare?

I care. I like them bare.
Then I can see all of them
There is to see.

With leaves they lose
The touch of individuality.
All oaks look somewhat the same to me.

Now I see the struggle, strife,
The very battles of life.
All can be seen - each hurt not healed.

Like all of us the trees reflect,
And like the trees we hide each speck,
And grow thick leaves - hide needs unmet.

What would life be
If you could see
All of me...like the tree?

Of course, 'tis true, like me and you,
Very few really SEE the tree.
They just glance and hurry by...
sigh.

CHAPTER 4

QUIET TIMES,

NURTURING TIMES

In repentance and rest is your salvation, in quietness and trust is your strength.

~ ~ Isaiah 30:15

Nor hell nor heaven shall that soul surprise
who loves the rain
and loves his home
And looks on life with quiet eyes.

~ ~ Frances W. Shaw

I remember working in the garden as a child and perhaps it is those early memories that bring me the peace I feel when I'm in my garden today. In a garden I feel shut off from the real world and transported to a quiet world where struggles and war cease for a few minutes. It is more than the satisfaction with the results of my labors that I am speaking of. Surely the flowers are beautiful and the vegetables tasty, yet for me it's the "doing" in the garden that I treasure most. I recall as a child trying to learn the difference between weeds and carrots, and how I once pulled out a whole row of carrots and had to re-plant each one back in the soil. This memory lingers after nearly half a century, and carries with it the old feeling of satisfaction in knowing those carrots finally grew to completion in spite of my fumbling.

In the spring we would plan and daydream, pouring over the catalogues and visualizing our gardens looking exactly like the ones in the pictures. Seed sowing is such an act of faith; the whole procedure is filled with wonderful hopes and expectations.

We always had a beautiful flower garden made up largely of plants exchanged with neighbors. I got to know the neighbors by the plants they shared, and whenever we went to visit friends and neighbors we always took some fresh flowers from the garden. I don't remember ever knowing first names. It was always "Mr." and "Mrs." My, how times have changed!

Gardens bring people together at a very basic level and are enriching for all involved. I think those who have known gardens intimately have a priceless heritage. My father, at the age of 85, was still getting enjoyment out of working the soil, planting, nurturing his foliage, and picking his strawberries.

Life today is so busy and harried, but, even if the garden can only be a small one, it is worth the time and energy required and can be a wonderful learning experience, especially for children. Besides learning the joy of sharing through the abundance from our garden, we also learned the value of quiet reflection. The saying "A person is closer to God in a garden than anywhere else on earth" is powerful and accurate. It is to this serene place where life flourishes that I now turn to unravel intricate matters that wound or perplex me, and to gain the strength to face crisis and sorrow. It is in a garden, where all is still, that we can feel God's spirit guiding us. And it seems the garden never fails the one who plants, nurtures, and tends it.

* * * * *

When I think back to some of the softer moments of my childhood, I also think of "home places." Home places are homes that have been in the family for generations; places where we can relax, be uninhibited, and be loved and accepted for who we are; where the screen door slams all summer long as children run in and out, and freshly baked breads and pies send delicious aromas into the fall air. It seems today's culture is so mobile, almost nomadic in lifestyle, that we've lost a great deal. We wander the earth, settling here for a while, there for a while, and it is becoming harder and harder to have a genuine home place, even in memory.

There were several home places for me. One was my grandma and grandpa's farm up north just outside of Fergus Falls, Minnesota. I remember the 12-hour trip in our '36 Chevy. There was no heater in that car, so, when we arrived, my grandma would set us on the oven door of the old wood stove to warm us up. She would also feed us freshly baked cinnamon rolls and fresh creamy milk from the cows. Once warmed, in body and spirit, we were off to play - swinging in grandpa's hammock, or making a playhouse in the plum thicket, using chickens as our children.

Then there was the place where I grew up in Ceresco township, ten miles from Madelia. It had been in the family for 90 years and my dad had been born in the upstairs bedroom. It was in that room that my sister and I slept and where I drew pictures in the frost on the windows. I thought all windows were for frost drawings until years later when I was invited to stay overnight at my friend's house. They had central heating and the upstairs was as warm as the downstairs, so no frost could form on the windows. It was there that I discovered the emptiness of frostless windows.

Our house was heated by a wood burning stove which during the night would go out. Every morning I'd hear my father starting the wood stove in the kitchen, then my mom would call us down for breakfast. In the winter we'd bring our clothes downstairs and get dressed in front of the stove where it was warmer. Then it was my job to make the toast. We'd put a grate on the stove and I'd put 7-9 slices of bread on it, watch so they didn't burn, then turn them over. If a piece burned I'd just scrape the burnt part off and we'd eat it anyway.

There was no heat in our upstairs. There was a register on the bathroom floor, just an opening, so the excess heat from the downstairs could drift up to the bathroom. There were three bedrooms upstairs: My brothers, Keith and Jerry, each had their own room, and my sister Kay and I shared one. Downstairs there was one bedroom where my parents slept, a living room and a dining room combined, and a kitchen. We later remodelled, adding a sun porch on the front of the house, a bathroom downstairs, and oak floors in the living/dining room. I remember the carpenter saying to my mother how lucky she was to have such a nice house while her children were young enough to enjoy it. He said he never had the time or money to fix up his own house.

We lived at the end of a long driveway almost a quarter mile long. Each morning we walked to the end of the drive to meet the school bus. At the end of the day, when we were dropped off, we would often smell bread baking and we'd run home to get it fresh out of the oven.

Until I was in the fourth grade we went to school in a one-room schoolhouse, three miles away. The school was heated by a big wood burning stove in one corner and there was no running water. We drank water from a pail with a dipper. At noon the oldest boy went across the road to the neighbor's to get a fresh pail of water. It was at this same neighbor's home that the teacher stayed during the week. The schoolhouse had no bathroom so, winter or summer, we had to go outside to the outhouse. Sometimes, if it was a beautiful spring day, I'd spend an extra long time on my way to the outhouse and back. In the winter I always moved fast.

I loved the country school because I could listen when the older children did their lessons, so I learned a lot more than what my class was learning. Of course there were only two children in my class - my first cousin and I.

Summers were especially fun once school was out. Mornings were for getting the farm work done. In the afternoon we would ride our bikes to the neighbor's, or we would play in our oat bin. Rainy days were spent pretending in the wonderful wood playhouse that my grandpa built. Other times we might walk across the creek to my Aunt Alverta's to help her for the afternoon since she had no children of her own to do chores.

Sometimes, on a hot summer day, we swam and splashed for endless hours in the creek. When we were younger, my mom would take along a magazine and go with us to watch us swim. The creek wasn't very deep so when we were older we were allowed to go alone. Often our cousins would walk over from their side of the creek to meet us. The story is told of the time the current was so strong it swept away the top of my cousin's bikini and she had to stay in the water until her brother brought her a new top.

In the spring we all enjoyed walking in the woods and picking wild flowers. I still remember the smell of new life breaking through the recently thawed forest floor. In the fall we crunched through crispy leaves gathering walnuts in gunny sacks, which we then brought up to the house for the breads my mother would bake in the winter.

For holidays we always got together with our aunts, uncles, and cousins, and the families took turns entertaining. The four families lived within a two mile radius on adjoining farmlands. It was a lot like a clan. We also all went to the same church, 14 miles away in Garden City. Church didn't get out till noon and then we had to drive home in that '36 Chevy, so we were always very hungry at the end of the 45 minute drive. Sometimes, if we stopped for gas, we might get a special treat of an ice cream cone or a candy bar. It was great fun being with my cousins; even going to church took on the aura of family fun time.

When we weren't playing we were learning the many farm and home skills necessary for our existence, either through the 4-H which we all belonged to, or at my mother's side. She taught me to sew on the old treadle sewing machine and she was as particular in this as she was in everything. If something was sewn crooked she made me take a pin and pull it out and do it over. I learned to be an excellent seamstress. She also taught me how to cook and to bake breads and pies.

When I was young we didn't have most of the modern conveniences we have today, so chores took longer. For instance, we did not have a power lawn mower. We had a push mower that we took turns with because it was so hard to push. It seemed to take forever to cut the grass. I remember how on hot summer days, after my turn pushing, I'd go inside and sit in front of our only fan, hoping to cool off before it was my turn again. The fan, also, was unlike the fans of today. It was black, about 12" around, and the cord was terribly frayed so we had taped it with black electrical tape. It ran this way for years, whirring noisily as it vibrated on its base, cooling many grateful faces.

In retrospect, I think teaching us to work together as a family and have us feel that we were important to the prosperity of the garden, the home, and the farm was a valuable lesson. It taught us responsibility and the pride and satisfaction that go with hard won success. We worked far more than we played, but I believe it was well worth it. Sometimes today I see children who are not expected to help with family chores at all, and I feel that is detrimental to their self-esteem, for where then do they find the values and hardships to shape their lives? We were never allowed to watch T.V. if there was work to do, and even though I was sometimes afraid of my parents' wrath, I also remember the many good times; at bedtime when they read us stories from our bible story book, and the times when we played the piano and sang songs in the parlor. Life was hard for all of us and money was tight, but we were taught God would take care of us and, certainly in that home place, He never failed.

Years later when we were grown and my brother moved there, he put pigs in the playhouse. I was furious, but my mother said it wasn't any of my business anymore. That home place was never the same after that. My brother remodeled it and made it bigger and, for me, it lost its charm...except in memory.

As an adult, my home place was in Linden Township where we came right after our honeymoon. It was there that our first child was born and our sixth, and all those in between. It was also there that the children's father and his father before him lived. This was Luther's home for 48 years, from infancy through adulthood, and it was his home with me and the children until his death.

That 400 acre farm had been in Luther's family since 1885, and the house built in 1911. The story is told that the night the family moved in, they were so glad to be warm after living in the log cabin, they built a fire so hot it charred the rafters in the basement. To this day you can see where the flames leapt up. From generation to generation that story has been passed on, each generation adding its own version, thus deepening the special quality of that home place.

Home places, the most intimate places in the world, are not always about buildings, but about the emotional states that exist among the families that live in buildings. In a larger sense, as Christians we are all members of the same family, the same home place. John 15:4 says, "Remain in me, and I will remain in you. No branch can bear fruit by itself; it must remain in the vine. Neither can you bear fruit unless you remain in me."

This year, seemingly a lifetime later, my husband, Fred, and I moved to a new home and, as beautiful as the building is, I wonder if it will ever be anybody's "home place." Will the neighbors ever refer to this as the Dauer farm? It takes many years of love, care, joys, and tears to create an authentic home place. So far the only part of this place that feels like home is the strawberry bed, for it is there that my father, long since dead, seems still to be tilling the soil, finding big, juicy worms for fishing, picking strawberries, and conversing with me as I work.

HOME PLACES

Lord, make this house a home place
Where those who come will say
There's something here that feels good,
And makes them want to stay.

Let those who come and fill our beds
Be filled with love You give,
So when they leave this home place,
They'll know with us You live.

Lord, make this house a home place
For the children who come here,
So when they grow and leave us,
They will do so without fear.

Let "Welcome" and "We love you"
Be the messages we give,
So all will want to share this place
As long as we shall live.

CHAPTER 5

SEEDS OF DEVOTION, HARVEST OF JOY

Train a child in the way he should go, and when he is old he will not turn from it.

~ ~ Proverbs 22:6

My first shock of married life came at 5:30 in the morning, the day after our wedding. We were honeymooning at a resort in northern Minnesota and it was just beginning to get light. I said to Luther, my husband, "Let's get up, it's time to go fishing." Sleepily, he said, "At this time of the morning? I'm certainly not going fishing, I don't even like to fish." I couldn't believe my ears.

We had never talked about it but I just assumed all men liked to fish. All the men and boys in my family had fished since they were old enough to hold a pole, and I always joined them. I had been going fishing with my father practically all my life. My mother was probably jealous of that, but she never wanted to go fishing. She hated those smelly fish. My dad and I always prepared the fish for cooking, then she would fry them.

As an adult, when we went up north to my mother's parents' place, I'd leave the kids with my mother and my aunt while I went fishing with my dad. They would prepare a nice dinner and then expect us to come home at noon to eat. If the fish were biting, we didn't always come and that irritated my mother.

My brothers wouldn't let me go fishing with them unless I picked up the worms. First we would find a five-tine pitch fork. My brother would then dig up a fork-full of dirt and I'd have to break up the dirt clumps and catch the worms before they crawled away. I did this by closing my eyes and grabbing quickly. Sometimes we went on the manure pile and got white grubs. I hated picking up those grubs. They were fat and white and ugly, but they were good for catching certain kinds of fish.

I liked fishing even better than gardening, and I always knew fishing season was open when the catfish started to bite in the river below our house. Fishing was an important part of my life and nothing, not even marriage, was going to change that.

Every morning of our honeymoon, I got up alone, got the boat in the water and went fishing while Luther slept. That pattern continued our entire married life. Often I would take the children and my parents and we'd go to my Aunt and Uncle's place where my mother would take care of the children, and my dad and I would go fishing. There is in fishing something that settles the soul.

We cut our honeymoon short because it was time to fill the silo and Luther thought he should be home to help. We returned home to the big thirteen-room home of my in-laws and began married life on the farm.

The house was huge. The upstairs had seven bedrooms. I was sure we'd never be able to fill them up, but as it turned out, with seven bedrooms and six children, all the rooms quickly filled. When we first moved there, however, each of the bedrooms was perfectly empty except for a bed and a dresser. The closets were empty except for a few hangers. My mother-in-law, Adeline, lived by the old adage, "a place for everything and everything in it's place." Her mother had been a terrible housekeeper, so she was just the opposite. Everything in her home was sparse, neat, and tidy. I, however, took after my mother who never threw anything away. The result of these divergent lifestyles was that I felt a constant stress to be something I was not.

The house had two entrances, one of which was through the back door to a small washroom with two sinks. I had never before seen two sinks side by side. The washroom led into a huge kitchen with a screened in porch attached, where there was also an entrance. You walked through the kitchen into a large dining room which had a four-unit bay window with a southern exposure. The ceilings were ten feet high and there were transom windows above the doors. My first impression of the old homestead had been that it looked more like a hotel than a house; it reminded me of the hotels on Gun Smoke. Once we had a baby sitter who asked us what the house was "before it was a house."

Also in the dining room there was beautifully carved woodwork, about a foot and a half wide, and a plate rail that ran the entire perimeter of the room. There were two built in china cabinets and two beautiful, floor-to-ceiling, sliding doors to the parlor. The doors were kept closed in the winter to conserve heat, except on Sunday. On Saturday nights in winter, Adeline would open them so we could sit in the parlor on Sunday.

In the parlor, besides the doors opening to the dining room, there were doors that opened to the den, which had been converted to a bedroom for Grandpa. Adeline's father, who was about 90 years old and hard of hearing, also lived with us. He could no longer maneuver steps, thus the bedroom downstairs.

If you walked on through the parlor, there was a foyer with large pillars and an open staircase, and a door that opened onto a front porch with large southern style pillars and a balcony directly above the porch. Originally this had been the main entrance, but over the years farmhands, family, guests, and even strangers came to the back door.

This was the arrangement I returned from the honeymoon to find: Orlando and Adeline had the central master bedroom upstairs. Grandpa was directly below them and would knock on the ceiling with his cane if he needed anything during the night. We were one door away in the guest room.

Every morning, at around 7:00 A.M., Luther's father, Orlando, would stand at the bottom of the stairs and call out, "Luther, time to get up!" I'm sure that was exactly how it had been for years.

We lived this way for about nine months. The second month of our marriage I became very ill. I eventually went to the doctor and explained that I had the flu and I wasn't getting better; I wasn't able to keep down any food. He asked me if it was possible I was pregnant. I said I supposed it was possible, but I'd never even thought of that. He determined that was the problem.

I hated throwing up with what seemed like a house-full of people. Often I would go to my mother's house during the day, and then come home at night when Luther was home. I especially hated having to go by the master bedroom on my way to throwing up in the bathroom. Finally, just before our first child, Jeffrey, was born, Adeline and Orlando moved eight miles away, although Orlando still came to help Luther every morning, and still shouted upstairs if we weren't up yet.

When Jeffrey was three months old I had a miscarriage. The doctor fitted me for a diaphragm, but I got pregnant again when Jeffrey was eight months old. I gained 42 pounds during that pregnancy and Billy weighed 9 pounds 8 ounces. I again tried a diaphragm and gel, but when Billy was 11 months old, I was pregnant again.

Jeffrey was a very active child, but Billy was very quiet and would sit in his highchair for hours, eating Cheerios and watching me work. Three weeks before the next baby was born, Jeffrey had his third birthday and was playing on a swing, when he fell and broke his leg. We had only the one bathroom upstairs, so I had to carry him up there, cast and all, pregnancy and all, when he needed to use it. It was then I decided we needed a downstairs bathroom more than we needed two sinks. We threw out one of the sinks and made a very tiny bathroom out of the old washroom.

What I remember best about my third son's, Kenneth's, birth was that I had my parents over for dinner that day and my mother asked me when I thought the baby would be born. I said, "Probably tonight." I was having labor pains in the kitchen, then I'd take the food to everyone in the dining room, and go back to the kitchen to have more pains. I never told anyone I was in labor. I went to the hospital at 5:30 p.m. and he was born at 10:30 p.m. It was a normal delivery and he was born sucking his thumb. None of my other children ever sucked their thumbs, but I decided it was his thumb and if he wanted to suck it, that was fine. He quit when he began school. Kenneth was strong willed and inquisitive. His was a very active childhood. I still feel guilty about his childhood because I was so busy and he was so full of life and so full of questions. When he was only 7 1/2 months old I was pregnant again. This time I didn't want anyone to know it; I was too embarrassed. I didn't go out often and I was, again, very sick. With Kenneth I'd been sick only the first four months, but now with this one, as with the earlier two, I was sick the entire pregnancy. I was still vomiting the night before I delivered.

Not anyone, not even my mother, knew how sick I was. I didn't let anyone know. Good girls did not complain, nor did they appear to have problems, or look anything less than perfectly happy. I made all my maternity clothes, lots of them, so I always looked nice. I also had my hair done every week. It was important to me that I looked good and not get sympathy for being sick. It was years later that I became aware of always feeling sorry for pregnant women when I saw them. I had never been overly thrilled to be pregnant and, underneath, I probably wanted sympathy so much it frightened me and I had to hide those feelings. Seeing other pregnant women would trigger my deep needs, so then I gave them the sympathy I'd always wanted.

I finally realized that sometimes women are actually happy to be pregnant, and don't need or want my sympathy.

But there I was, pregnant again. I had three little boys ages three, two, and one, and this time the doctor assured me the baby was a girl. I had a new doctor, so the baby was born in a different hospital, in New Ulm, 13 miles from my home. My son was born at 10:30 a.m. on January 19, 1965. I had no boy's names picked out.

After the delivery I was back in my room talking to my roommate, when she seemed to be getting farther and farther away. Then my voice started sounding strange, like I could hardly hear the words and they didn't seem to be coming from me. I was in a room on the third floor and I remember there were sliding windows. I had the impression I could just walk out the window and not fall. I was sort of floating. I could see the doctor there and Luther came and the priest was praying over me even though I wasn't Catholic. Several nuns were also gathered around.

Breathing was becoming just too much work. I remember hearing the doctor say, "Breathe, just breathe!" But I was too tired. They hooked me up to several machines and gave me blood. There was the sound of music all around and a beautiful light, and lots of people. I asked someone if it was alright if I died. I was told it was alright if I wanted to walk out the window, but if I did, it would close and I wouldn't be able to come back. He said it really wasn't fair to leave Luther with four little boys to raise. I remember thinking that death wasn't scary at all, nothing like I'd imagined it.

When I came to someone was asking me if I wanted to hold my baby, and sometime later this nameless child was at my breast. Somehow my parents and Luther's parents had come to the hospital. Throughout all the confusion and eeriness, I think I heard my mother crying and Luther's parents praying. When I was fully aware once again, I was glad I had stayed around so I could help raise the children.

Luther and I always wanted only four children. He and I both were the youngest of four. Now we had our fourth and thought our family was complete. We named him Miles Orlando, after each of our fathers.

In retrospect, I believe my denial of my disappointment that the baby was a boy may have caused me to go into shock. I was so disappointed, but wouldn't cry because I didn't want anyone, especially the baby, to know how disappointed I was.

I always felt when my last two children were born, they were like a second family with a different mother because I felt so changed after that; it was always "the four boys" and "Mary and Mitch." That experience became one of the turning points of my life: I was no longer afraid of death.

I believe Luther and I did an excellent job of parenting, considering some of the problems we had in our marriage. When we married, we basically knew nothing about how to make a marriage work. Our pastor gave us a test before we married to see if we were compatible and it showed that we were almost too much alike; the pastor was afraid we'd have a boring life. Somehow we muddled through, and now here I was at 24 years of age, the mother of four sons ages four, three, two, and an infant.

We lived in a small, rural community just two miles from Linden Lutheran Church. My husband's great grandfather, Pedar Thormodson, was one of three officers when the church was founded in 1858. There is a big statue with all the founders' names on it in the cemetery that surrounds the church. Luther's family is buried right next to the sidewalk and Luther's stone is there also. It was hard having to walk by it on the way to church every Sunday after he died.

During that first ten years of marriage, life on the farm was one of tremendous family involvement. My parents lived 14 miles in one direction and Luther's parents lived eight miles in the other. Every day for at least ten years my father-in-law was at our house by 7 A.M. and he stayed until 5 P.M., helping Luther in the fields.

We had 400 acres of land, with 20 acres of woods and a lake. We raised hay and soybeans and corn. We also milked cows and raised pigs for the first ten years of our married life. We had what is called a "farrow to finish" operation with the pigs. The sows would have the baby pigs and then we raised them up to market weight and sold them.

When Luther finished his work in the fields, sometimes he would help his brother. Of course, sometimes his brother also helped him if he needed it. Luther helped me with the children as much as he could, but usually was too busy outdoors.

My chore inside was to prepare dinner at noon, which always consisted of meat and potato's, gravy, vegetable, and salad. Most of the time we had pie for dessert. There were also morning and afternoon lunches expected.

I remember many times trying to nurse the baby, supervise the older children, and answer the phone, all while stirring the food on the stove and planning this meal and the next. Having any time or thoughts to myself was out of the question. Most of the time I was too busy even to acknowledge that I might have needs or an inner life of my own.

When Miles was three months old I was so overworked and tired that I remember wishing I could go to the hospital just for a rest. It seemed life was no more than an endurance test, the goal being to survive until the children became adults. I also recall wondering if, in my whole life, I would ever not be dead tired. I couldn't even nurse the baby in peace because all the others wanted to sit on me, climb on me, and talk to me as soon as I tried. When I was a little girl my mother always told us if we weren't good she would lose her mind and have to go to the mental institution in St. Peter, Minnesota. I wasn't sure what that meant, to lose one's mind or have a nervous breakdown, but I was now beginning to wonder if that's what was happening to me.

The pressures in me built and the exhaustion was overwhelming. I finally went to my doctor and told him I was afraid I'd have a nervous breakdown. He assured me that what I needed was a vacation, and he gave me the book Peace With God, by Billy Graham. I took his advice and, with the baby and the book, went to visit my favorite aunt for a week. Today I know that it is only as I live in harmony with myself that I can feel God's peace within and can express His love in my life. Back then I didn't know that. I read the book, had a nice visit with my aunt, then returned to my own frantic life, having learned or resolved nothing. I felt isolated and overwhelmed. My days were busy and full, but not fulfilling. I continued doing all I could do for everyone except myself, and learning as I went along, by trial and error, the best ways to function and survive.

One of the things I learned was that when I was upset and wanted the babies to hurry and nurse, then go to sleep, they never did. But when I was relaxed and didn't care how much time it took, they usually went to sleep easily, without finishing nursing. I believe that not only did the milk not flow as freely when I was nervous or tense, but that the makeup of the milk was different. I have nothing scientific with which to back this up, but I know that the chemical makeup of tears that are cried in joy differs from those cried in sorrow and those from peeling an onion. So, it makes sense to me that the chemical makeup of breast milk also changes with the mother's mood.

When my babies were irritable, I learned to look into myself to see what anxieties they might have been sensing in me. I need to emphasize that this has very little to do with outside, observable behavior. It has to do with gut level feelings, the kind we are often unaware of from moment to moment.

When I got the three toddlers and the baby dressed and ready for church, if I remained inwardly calm and didn't raise my voice, by the time we got there the children would cuddle up to me and be content. However, if I was rushed or upset on the inside, even if I didn't show it on the outside, they were terrible. They wiggled and teased each other and competed for attention. Then I would become even more upset and vow I'd never take them again. But once I learned the secret of this emotional stability transference trick, I was relatively sure they would probably attend church for the rest of their lives and never really know why, except that at some deep level it felt good. They are now ages 21 to 31 and, of the six, two are in full time Christian service, and all are very active in church.

I also found that when I took the children to my mother's and wanted them to be especially quiet, they were not quiet at all. They seemed to become irritable and impossible. The harder I'd try to keep them quiet, because noise bothered my mother, the more unmanageable they would become. Sometimes they would be just fine on the way to her house, but the moment we got there it was mayhem.

Children seem to have built-in sensors; they are much more attuned to people than we give them credit for. They can tell if they are enjoyed or merely tolerated. My mother was much less patient with children than I, and the children knew it. Her view of children was that they should be seen and not heard, and barely acknowledged. I didn't feel that children needed to occupy center stage all of the time, but I did feel they were people to be respected. I taught them that when an adult conversation was going on they were to play elsewhere. I also felt that, as grandparents, my parents could have talked to the kids a little and shown them some love and acknowledged their presence before shoving them in the corner or rushing them outside. But I was still trying to win my mother's approval, so I didn't voice my beliefs. I thought maybe if I could prove what a great mother I was by displaying the well-behaved, quiet children I had raised, I would finally feel her love and approval. Of course that never happened. It never does.

When my dad was alone with us he was different. He always had time for the kids. He hugged them, just as he had me when I was young, and he told them what good kids they were. He had a huge garden and would let the older ones go with him to pick strawberries or, later in the season, pick up the potatoes he dug. They would help carry the potatoes to the root cellar for the winter.

When I took the kids fishing, Grandpa always went along. He would have the worms ready by the time we picked him up. Or, if we went to a bait shop, since I didn't have a lot of extra money, he would pay for the minnows and buy a treat for the kids. Often it was ice cream and the kids would be a mess before we ever began fishing, but no one cared. We'd sit on the bank of the lake enjoying the ice cream, the blue skies, and the birds, while we talked about life.

When we took the children to Luther's parents' house, however, it was an entirely different story. His father was the one who rarely played with the children, and his mom was wonderful with them. They knew she loved children and would be happy to see them. She would greet them each by name and show them to the toy box where she kept coloring books and clay and all kinds of magical things. Luther and I had the youngest grandchildren and I felt like they were the favorites. Looking back, I imagine all of the grandchildren felt special to her.

We went to the same church as Luther's parents, and his mom would let one or two of the kids sit with her. She always took gum and gave them a stick during the sermon. She was a kind, loving, patient person, and I loved her a lot. We were so different and, even though she didn't understand me, I knew she loved me anyway. She never tried to change any of us or tell us what to do. She often baby sat for the children, and while they were with her, their behavior was fun and relaxed. They always looked forward to those visits.

On the way home from Grandma Thormodson's house the kids slept peacefully. On the way home from my parent's house and a visit with my mother, even if they had been relatively quiet while there, they would be fighting and teasing each other. By the time we left I always had a headache. It was like having a kettle of boiling water with the lid on and the minute it was removed, all hell broke loose.

I eventually gained confidence in my ability to comfort crying babies by paying attention to my own level of anxiety. I remember being at a church camp where a mom was having a terrible time with her baby crying during a lecture. I offered to hold the baby and did this during the lectures for several days. I would hold the baby close and pat its back and silently say, "What a beautiful baby you are. Just go to sleep. God loves you and so do I." It felt like I could actually feel a flow of energy from me to the child. I admit this is often more difficult to do with our own babies because we are always aware of time constraints and the unending responsibilities we have...24 hours a day without respite. This brings its own stress which we may believe we're handling well, or hiding and keeping to ourselves, but which our children detect at a very deep level.

Today I am a massage therapist and I seem to be able to transfer that same energy between me and the person to whom I'm giving a massage. Clients often say I have a healing touch because my hands are very warm and strong. My husband is always telling me how much he loves to hold me or be held by me. He says he can feel the energy flow and it feels like it recharges his battery. He feels nourished just from being held. Relaxed, loving touching is such a basic human need and such a life-giving gift, yet it is one that is so sadly neglected. I used to dream about my mother holding and hugging me, but she was always too busy. I've ached for it all my life. I have had psoriasis, an itchy and annoying skin disease, for years, as has my mother. Perhaps it's related to the lack of touching in my early years. I believe my mother also experienced this lack in her childhood. This feels very symbolic: Itching to be touched, hugged, to experience the life-giving energy of another person.

Babies especially, it seems to me, being so fresh to the world and defenseless, are highly attuned to this energy when it's flowing freely, and are painfully aware of its absence when it's not. When I nursed my babies and was happy and relaxed it was like no other experience on earth, and the contentment and bonding we shared during those moments were priceless.

* * * * *

It was after Miles was born that I decided, realistically, that I had to do something. Even though I believed children were gifts from God, so are the peace and contentment that allow for adequate, loving child-rearing. So I started taking birth control pills. I took them for about three years until I had side effects and then I quit taking them. At that point I decided to try the rhythm method, which my Catholic doctor referred to as Vatican roulette.

It was about this time that I read an article on how to choose the sex of your child. I don't recall much about it except that it had to do with the time of the month you got pregnant determining the sex of the baby. I had mononucleosis at the time and knew it wasn't the best time to get pregnant, but I had always wanted a girl. This desire was so strong in me that I tricked Luther into believing it was a safe time for intercourse, and I became pregnant immediately and was delighted because I believed it would be a girl. Miles was then four years old.

When it was time to go to the hospital, I was concerned because they couldn't detect a heartbeat and I hadn't felt the baby move the last few weeks. Even though we'd never shared it, both Luther and I had been worried about the baby. Later Luther told me he had prayed for us every day as he was out working in the fields.

As soon as the baby's head emerged, the doctor said, "The cord is wrapped around the baby's neck..." He paused and then said, "...twice." He immediately cut the cord. When he told me it was a girl I said, "She's not breathing, is she?"

"No," he said, and immediately he and the nurses left with the baby to work on her in another room. This was before fathers were allowed in the delivery room, so I was left there all alone to wonder what was happening.

What seemed like an eternity passed before the doctor returned. He never assured me she was alright so I was relieved when, a few hours later, they brought her to me. She was a lovely baby. The doctor said it was a miracle she had lived, and we would have to keep a close check on her as she might be retarded. Mary grew up perfectly fine. The only problem she had was that she needed very strong glasses. Today she wears contact lenses.

I just loved raising Mary. The three boys were in school and on the day she was born, Miles, the youngest of the other four, started nursery school. I was so happy that I had time to nurse her, sing to her, and enjoy her in peace. She never had a bottle. I nursed her for nine months and then she drank from a cup.

After Mary was born I was still having trouble getting all my housework done and my doctor prescribed diet pills for the energy. Since Luther didn't like it if the house wasn't clean, and I never had the energy anymore to do the cleaning, I took the pills. The pills pepped me up to the extent that I was able to accomplish almost twice the work I could previously. Luther liked how efficient and tidy I had become. I now realize how dangerous and how foolish that was.

When Mary was about 18 months old I was sick with strep throat, hospitalized, and given strong medicine. They were afraid I had leukemia because my blood had too many red cells and hardly any white cells. They were going to do a bone marrow test, but then I started to improve and the doctor said it was just a massive virus. It also turned out that part of the problem was that I was pregnant with Mitchell.

Mitchell's was the only delivery I had without any medication and without an episiotomy. I hated the needles with the novocaine. The doctor thought it might be alright, but Mitchell was 8 pounds 9 ounces, and I ripped. The doctor sewed me up and I actually recovered much faster than I had from my other deliveries because I had fewer stitches.

Mitch was a delightful child. He had a smile for everyone and was very easy going. He and Mary got along very well and to this day are best friends.

I continued to take the diet pills for 12 years until the doctor who prescribed them died and no other doctor would fill the prescription. When I stopped taking them I just stopped. I didn't have any group help and I didn't tell anyone. When I was taking them I felt guilty about being on them, but I felt worse about having a messy house when I didn't take them. During all those years when the children were little, I rarely slept more than four hours. I'd work all day caring for them, take a pill, then work at night cleaning the house while the family slept.

Still, despite all the worries, messes, runny noses, scraped knees, and seemingly endless sleepless nights, we found that raising our children was a joyful experience and a true blessing from God.

A RAINY MONDAY NIGHT

It just occurred to me that maybe
What I want out of life is to just be;
Just be me and do my thing.
Perhaps even better without a gold ring.

Some people are made to enjoy
Being together all of the time.
I was made to need my space,
To think and love and set my own pace.

I love to be loved when I want to,
But when I don't I just say no.
I don't expect the other to change,
"To do my thing," the name of the game.

But inside I wonder if there's something wrong
That I always need to be so strong
And be in control and do it my way,
Rarely changing because of what others say.

Am I afraid to let others in
Because of the fear under my skin?
Do I hide out and just pretend
Because I'm afraid their love will end?

These are the questions that race through my mind,
Filling my life so I just don't have time
To stop and relax and just let life flow;
Always it seems I'm on the go.

Searching for something I haven't found.
What can it be? How does it sound?
What does love look like really up close?
Hurt is a strange thing, more dangerous than most.

Help me dear God to let Your love in.
Let me forget self so I may begin
To experience others as nothing to fear
As long as I know that Your love is here.

Help me love me, just as I am,
With all of my weakness, and all of my sin,
So that when I die others will know
By loving You is how we all grow.

CHAPTER 6

WINDS OF CHANGE

> There is a time for everything, and a season for every activity under heaven.
>
> ~ ~ Ecclesiastes 3:1

> Heaven from all creatures hides the book of fate.
>
> ~ ~ Alexander Pope

The early years of child-rearing, as the children grew beyond the infant stage, are a bit of a blur, but I do recall an incident in 1976 that was important to me. I was chairman of the county Mental Health Association and was teaching a course called Parent Effectiveness Training, and a new psychologist, certified in that area, came on staff. I met him to discuss some business and he said, "You must come from a very interesting family. I'd like to get to know you better." Later I came to realize that he was detecting my inner turbulence, conflict, anxiety, and fear. He also caught how frustrated and overwhelmed I was with my role as a full-time mother and wife. It was then he told me he had never met anyone with so much going for them who had such low self-esteem.

Those words were like manna from heaven to a person dying of starvation. I had been trying to survive my inner turmoil and aloneness by reading books...books about people whose lives appeared enriched and complete. In that way I was temporarily able to escape my own empty existence. But such books, in the end, only reinforced my negative self-image; they didn't touch my heart and they didn't heal. I was thirsting for happiness and peace of mind by looking for it in every book I could find, but I'd get lost in the words and die inside the pages.

While mothering brought me some of my greatest satisfaction, I knew that inside I was still empty. I'd learned enough relational skills to realize that intimacy could bring a certain amount of fulfillment, but I was lacking any real intimacy with my husband, and I had nowhere to turn to fill that void. Children cannot and should not be expected to fill a void, and my early religious training taught me that each of us is made with a hole that only God can fill. For many years I prayed, read the Bible, and lived a "good Christian life," trying to fill my gaping hole, but I was fundamentally unsuccessful.

Now, as my fifth grade teacher had so long ago, someone was again recognizing that there was more to me than I could acknowledge; more substance and more pain.

* * * * *

I began therapy shortly after that with the new psychologist, but I didn't begin for any of the right reasons. Rather, I rationalized that, as Chairman of the county Mental Health Association, and as a member of the State Mental Health Board, I should experience what happened when people came to the center for therapy. I began not because I thought I *needed* it, but so that I could be informed enough to help those who *did* need it. This was definitely to be a learning experience and an intellectual exchange only. I quickly learned, however, that I was one of "those" who needed it.

I recall saying in one of the first sessions, "I'm doing everything I know how to do: I go to church every Sunday, I belong to all the women's organizations, I teach Sunday school, I go to all of my children's activities...and I'm miserable. I don't know what is wrong with me." I then burst into tears.

When I regained my composure, I apologized for crying. You see, Luther didn't like it when I cried, so I'd cry only when I was alone. That had been going on for at least ten years. Luther said crying made him uncomfortable, and he thought women just used crying as a tool to manipulate men. I now know that many women are discouraged from experiencing their real emotions, and hence their real potential, by husbands who cannot handle honest emotions. So this sudden outburst with my (male) therapist left me feeling exposed and ashamed.

This time, however, my pain and tears fell on welcoming ears. My therapist accepted, even encouraged, my tears, and, for the first time in my life, they flowed freely. Even though it felt like they'd never stop, I didn't care. It felt good to cry, to release all the pent up feelings. This, finally, was the beginning of filling that empty place in my heart. It was the beginning of the healing process.

It took many long months before I finally trusted the therapist. It was two steps forward and one step backward all the way. I kept trying to heal myself, to look better on the outside than I was feeling on the inside, so that the therapist would like me. I wanted an equal relationship with him, but was far too disturbed for that to be. Unfortunately, I got a lot of reinforcement for my "craziness" from my friends. I could never be peaceful inside because the pain was too much to bear, so I attempted to cover up the pain by always being "up," jovial, on the go...traits all too often viewed as healthy, fun, and alive. I was never considered boring to my friends, but what they didn't know was that, inside, the pain was so bad, the only way I could numb it was with excessive talking and frenetic activity.

In therapy I eventually began to feel human again. I could just as well say that I began to *feel* at all for the first time in years. And since I had been shut down for so long, even the awful feelings that were emerging were better than nothing, and they were genuine feelings, not false as my mask of lightheartedness had been. It took a while, but I began to believe that the therapist liked me just the way I was and, even more importantly, he liked the parts of me I tried so hard to hide.

It was after about nine months of therapy that I wrote "The Rose." One morning I got up before anyone else and sat at my writing table in the early morning light. Suddenly the words just started flowing, as my tears had months before. There was a script running through my head and when I picked up my pen, the words tumbled quickly onto the paper. I felt compelled to write and the words just kept coming. I remember thinking, "Maybe this is just garbage and I'm wasting paper." I then looked at the front of the notebook and realized it had cost only 68 cents, so I thought, "If this is worthless, not much is lost."

I took "The Rose" to my next therapy session and read it to the therapist. Since he recognized himself as the gardener, he was moved. He wiped a tear from his eye and said, "I imagine we all want to be gardeners in someone's life." Later I read it to the toastmaster's club and received praise for it. My daughter, who was then about eight years old, also loved to have me read it to her. She told me recently that she was at least 16 before she even began to understand what it was really about. In college, years later, I had a bad experience when I shared it with my creative writing class and the professor said it was excellent, but it seemed a bit boastful to refer to one's self as a rose. I never again shared it until now.

As a natural extension of my therapy, I wanted Luther also to look inward and learn more about himself. However, he liked himself (or so he said) just the way he was, and he had no intention of looking inside. He said, "I don't care what is going on inside. I don't want to know." I think in some ways Luther hated the therapist for upsetting my view of myself and, therefore, our patterns of relating, but he just said, "Do your own thing and don't bother me." He said he didn't care what I did as long as I thought it helped and it didn't affect him.

I now realize that men usually handle emotions differently than women; they keep their sensitive side to themselves, and it is often so well hidden that they themselves are unaware of it. My confusion resulted from the fact that I had a father who often cried at beautiful, sad, or happy things. He was much more sensitive and freer with expressing that sensitivity than was my mother, who rarely cried. Luther's mom also shared her feelings, but his father didn't at all, nor did Luther. I believe that Luther didn't like to see me go through the pain of therapy, but he didn't know what to do to help me any more than I did, and his frustration and inability to be sensitive led him to become rather defensive and harsh.

I have read that when one person grows in a marriage and the other remains the same, the relationship suffers. The fact is, Luther liked me just the way I was before I started therapy. I had such low self-esteem that I'd do anything for anyone just to get a little praise. Now my new growth, and my beginning to feel like a worthwhile person in my own right, threatened the unconscious contract upon which our marriage was established. Before, it hadn't mattered who asked me to do something; if it was humanly possible I obliged.

My mother was especially good at getting me to do what she wanted. For example, she would call me up and ask me to take her 30 miles to Mankato to go shopping, because she didn't like to drive in Mankato. This meant I had to make arrangements with my mother-in-law to baby-sit, prepare dinner in advance for Luther and my father-in-law, dress the kids, pack their bottles and diapers, and haul them to their grandma's - all so I could spend several hours someplace I didn't want to be, while my work was not getting done at home. Yet it never occurred to me to say no. I can't blame my mother; it was always my choice to comply, and compliance was still high on my list of priorities. But now I was beginning to make different choices, ones that did not seem consistent with a compliant milquetoast, and it was threatening to Luther and, ultimately, to our marriage.

Now I began doing what I thought was best for me and I no longer bowed to everyone else's wishes. There was a time in therapy when I was actually very selfish, but I think that was necessary until I learned how to be more responsible with this new-found freedom. It was like learning how to live all over again, and it was not easy. All my life I'd had people telling me what to do and, even though I no longer wanted that, it was a big adjustment.

There were still times I wanted the therapist to tell me what to do, and he wouldn't, which was very frustrating. I rationalized this occasional need by believing there were good dictators and bad dictators, and I sometimes wanted him to be a good dictator. Having recently returned from a trip to Russia, I now see a parallel here; for over fifty years, the people of Russia (as have the people of all Communist-ruled societies) have had someone to tell them what to do. Now they are without that and are confused. They are predictably and necessarily shaky and unsure of their new-found freedom. A dictatorship in any form, gives structure to lives and relieves people of a certain amount of responsibility. However, I now see that all forms of dictating are destructive because they threaten to take away our dignity as human beings and turn us into helpless, dependent children.

Therapy helped me to realize that, besides wanting to be told what to do, there were many times when I told everyone else what to do and expected them to do it. I did this because I couldn't successfully run my own life, and when you can't run your own life you try to run everyone else's lives.

I was also very rigid back then, always on a timetable. When things didn't go the way I wanted them to, I either made them work or just walked out. Just like with my mother, everything was black and white, right and wrong. Understanding this helped me become much more flexible and forgiving.

It was at about this stage in therapy that I began to see that maybe, just maybe, my image of God was also faulty.

As a child, my idea of God was formed in my imagination by my mother's image of herself and, therefore, of her God. All my life I had thought I knew God. When I began therapy, I was sure God still talked to me and guided my decisions in life. But I learned that that God was not God at all. That God was what my mother created for me.

I was talking to my daughter recently and she recalled how, "Grandma always told me that God kept a check list of everyone and we got marks for being good or bad." She went on, "I never thought she really believed that." She then asked me if I thought Grandma still believed that. Yes, she still believes that, as, when I was growing up, I did. I never knew exactly what was supposed to happen when I was good, but I knew the bad always far outweighed any good in me and, therefore, God must not have liked me. I spent my life trying to get God and others to like me by doing or being anything and everything anyone wanted, and by being a "good Christian" so as not to receive any black marks.

In actuality, those black marks became more directly associated with my mother's anger than with a distant God; they once took the form of welts all over my body. This occurred when I was about five years old and my mother caught me masturbating. She took a belt and hit me on my legs, back, and bottom, leaving welts. Years later she apologized for that, but the damage had been done. I regularly received "lickings," as my dad called them, with hairbrushes, yardsticks, and rose tree branches. I was always made to find and cut the branch and bring it in for the whipping, so I made sure I found one with no thorns. When my mother whipped me with a stick, it usually broke, so it wasn't too bad. Rarely did I have to get another stick.

I hardly recall ever hearing my dad say I needed a licking. It was my mother who always told him to spank me, and because of that, I never really believed his heart was in it. The worst part of the pain was the anticipation. My mother would often tell me, "Just wait till your father gets home," or "Your father is going to hear about this." So for several hours I'd have to live with the fact that a licking was coming.

With my mother it was usually an open hand, a hair brush, or a branch or stick. My father used either a yardstick or his belt. He would come home and be happy to see me. He'd hug me, and then my mother would explain what I had done, and then he'd take me into their bedroom, take off his belt, and spank me on my bare bottom. The belt was folded in half and, if the buckle was in his hand, it didn't hurt as much as if the buckle was exposed. I think if it had been up to him, he would not have spanked me nearly so often. The hands used for my punishment were the same ones I loved so much when we did chores together and he would hold my little hand in his big, strong one.

I cried a lot when I was little and was often referred to as a cry-baby. To this day I dislike weeping willow trees because they remind me of my tears and pain. I was such a sensitive child I would only need to be told, not struck, for me to comply. Full compliance, however, was never possible under any circumstances because the "right" behavior or the "right" answer changed daily according to my mother's mood. I never knew how to be "good" at any given moment. It was only in retrospect, after the punishments, that I knew how I had failed, how I had "sinned," how bad I had been.

A couple of the misdeeds I can recall being punished for were picking an apple when it was green and eating it when I should have left it to ripen. Another time I ran on the cellar door at my piano teacher's house while my sister was taking her lesson, and it was disruptive. My cousin had been running with me, but I was the only one to be punished, which didn't seem fair.

Achievement was another area where I failed to meet expectations, and therefore "sinned." Again, whatever my accomplishments, they were never enough to please

Mother or God. Mother was, in this sense, God. She was sure she *knew* what God wanted. Everything was black and white, and she knew with certainty which was which in God's eyes. And, since she alone on earth seemed to know the crime, she was self-appointed to punish in the name of God. It never occurred to me the punishment might be unjust. I thought my parents were helping me so I would grow up to be a "good girl."

My mother is now 90 years old and I've tried many times to help her realize God doesn't keep a list. If He did we would all fall short of perfection and have countless black marks. However, when one has had so many years of conditioning, as my mother has had, change is indeed difficult.

One of the most difficult parts of therapy was forsaking that old image of God, for at first I was sure I would go to Hell if I ever questioned my religious beliefs. It was many months before I could let myself believe that the therapist wasn't being used by the devil to lead me astray. For me to finally realize that my mother was not God, and that God was far bigger, wiser, and more loving and accepting than she, created tremendous upheaval in my life and in my thinking.

I have read that when Stalin died in Russia, the saying "God is Dead" was common.

> When Kruschev exposed Stalin...it hit them as if they had been struck down by a train, shattering their beliefs to their very foundations, leaving them stunned at first, but then, later on open to new ways of thinking and more flexible than the generation that preceded them...
>
> "For those people, the Twentieth Congress was a shock, because, you know, Stalin was like God to them...It was as if they had lost their religion. You believe in Christ, or in Allah, or in Buddha, and all of a sudden something happens. Your whole life is changed and your beliefs are lost. And you are trying to look for something else to lean upon, some other foundation..."[1]

For me, my total dependence upon my mother was gone and, with it, the image of God she had ingrained in me. This was a loss that involved the core of my being. It left me shaken and frightened.

---

[1]Hedrick Smith, The New Russian, Avon Books, New York, 1991. Quotation from Roy Medvedv, in an interview with the author, October 9, 1989.

The danger with moving forward is always in wanting to return to the way things were, to past familiarity that held some semblance of security. I recall the story of the Israelites who wanted to go back to the Pharaoh and to Egypt. No matter how destructive a previous situation may have been, it was familiar. And, no matter how chaotic or painful, there's some predictability, some security, in familiarity. Perhaps that is also one reason people go back to abusive relationships. Little in life is as scary as the unknown. And I believe it's possible to be so mixed up that we may not only not recognize the difference, but, through conditioning, actually believe that bad feels good, that abuse feels like love.

Change is never easy, and the path is treacherous. With the guidance and support of my therapist, with fleeting flickers of hope, and with enormous trepidation, I continued.

Even though my husband and I were running into difficulties stemming from my growth, my relations with my children greatly improved as I continued in therapy. This was beneficial in and of itself, for how many of us wouldn't opt for better communication with our children. But it also gave me positive reinforcement and reason to continue the arduous task of looking inward.

One particular incident with one of my children comes to mind. On Mitch's first day at kindergarten, he was caught running down the hall to the bus. The principal called me and said, "Mrs. Thormodson, Mitch was running in the hall. When I grabbed him he tried to kick me. He was crying hysterically. I found his sister in second grade and she got Mitch on the right bus. Mitch may be a little upset when he gets off the bus and I just wanted you to know what happened."

My parents happened to be visiting that day, and they overheard the conversation. Grandma's immediate solution was to spank Mitch when he got home for kicking the principal. About this time the boys arrived and Mitch ran upstairs as fast as he could and hid under the farthest corner of the bed. My dad calmly said, "If that is the worst thing he ever does in his life, to run in the hall, it won't be too serious." I thought of that many times in future years.

I prepared lunch for my parents and sent them on their way as quickly as possible, no longer feeling I needed to adhere to my mother's views or let her interfere with my interactions with my children. I then went up to Mitch and held him on my lap while he sobbed his little heart out.

I recently talked to him about this incident and, at 22 years of age, he still recalls it vividly. He said, as he had that day, it was such a long way to the bus and he knew if the bus left without him, he couldn't walk home because it was too far and he didn't know the way. So, he ran to catch the bus. His fear then turned to panic when he was stopped, and he kicked. His lashing out was a survival instinct, no different than that of a trapped animal. I am still sad when I think of how frightened he had been. What a terrible mistake it would have been to spank him.

As I felt Mitch's kindergarten pain, I recalled something that happened when I was in the first grade. It was a little country school and as we were playing ball on the playground, the ball went out into the road. I saw a big gravel truck coming, and in my little mind, if the truck hit the ball it would have tipped over, so I thought that by running after the ball and retrieving it, I was doing something noble. Well, the man in the truck got out and told me, in furious tones, never to do that again because he nearly hit me. When I got home I was spanked for my terrible, irresponsible behavior.

As I remembered this incident, it dawned on me that, just as my image of God had been faulty, maybe I'd also had a distorted view of my childhood. Maybe it hadn't been perfect after all.

* * * * *

Therapy opened up so many new vistas for me. As I was able to see that my childhood was far less than ideal, as are most, I began to let go of a lot of old anger and fears. I still felt the emptiness, but I now had hope for the future and was beginning to have confidence in myself. I decided what I needed was a college degree. The advice of the fifth grade teacher and the affirmation from the psychologist remained in my mind, encouraging me, and I thought a degree and a career outside the home was what was missing.

My youngest child was now in school all day. I was afraid if I waited until all the children left home before I started back to college, I might begin to resent them. I would feel like a martyr, like I'd given my life for them and never done what I needed most to do for myself, for the health of my own soul. I reasoned that if I started college then, by the time all my children had graduated from high school, I'd have my master's degree.

I began my freshman year of college in the fall of 1976, and the following March my therapist moved to a different state. For me it was as though the lights had been turned on in my life and I had begun seeing for the first time: Seeing who I really was, seeing vast potential, and seeing all of life with new eyes. Now, suddenly, the lights were shut off again. I had started to see my primary family as dysfunctional, and I was learning to leave behind many old ways, but I did not yet have a new support system with which to buffer this painful separation. I felt abandoned and terrified. The light was gone and I felt I was in limbo, unable to move forward alone. Yet I also knew that I could never go back to the way it had been, ever again. I had seen the light and I could no longer embrace the darkness as my friend.

I hated the therapist for abandoning me. For a year I wandered around in a fog, barely surviving. I often thought about suicide, but I didn't know if I'd go to Hell for that, and I didn't want to abandon my children.

In the therapy relationship, my emotional hunger was just beginning to be satisfied. I was beginning to learn to trust. Now I felt like a baby who had been weaned prematurely. I couldn't yet feed myself and I had no one to teach me.

It took me a few years to get over this "abandonment." What kept me going, what helped me to survive, was college. I took 28 credits the first quarter I was there. All of them were senior courses, but I got special permission even though I was only a Freshman. I went to school three days a week from ten in the morning to ten at night. I got six A's and a B that quarter. I also team-taught a Human Relations course for Independent Study. I drove 60 miles round trip every day that I went to school.

I loved college, but I lived in two different worlds. One was at school where I was listened to and encouraged, and the other was at home where I did all my work and tried to keep everything running smoothly, but without much emotional support.

Many years later I had a chance to see my therapist again. We hadn't seen each other for 12 years, and during all that time I had felt that he had left *because* of me; that's how low my self-esteem had been. We talked about his leaving and he explained that he hadn't planned it that way, but circumstances were such that he'd had to relocate. That was a turning point for me, for once again I was able to hear the sound advice he shared with me, and I could let go of the anger and hurt. Our paths have not crossed since then except for occasional letters. However, my decisions in life are influenced daily by his presence. I could tell you what he told me fifteen years ago more surely than I could tell you what was said by someone yesterday.

Perhaps, symbolically, it was like Jesus explaining that He had to leave, so that the Holy Spirit could come down and be with the disciples. For me to grow into my own person and become the Rose within, the Gardener had to leave me. The critical part that needed to be done, I had to do on my own; to re-claim and integrate the painful parts of my past, and no longer use all my energy to deny or hide the truth.

Those who have experienced the darker sides of their own nature and of life know that if we can work through our projections and paranoia, we will emerge with a much deeper awareness of all of life because of the difficulties we have endured. Reading about poverty is not the same as living in poverty, and if one emerges from poverty, the experience is never totally forgotten. It's the same with any hardships or emotional struggles. People who have endured hardships have a far greater potential for a better understanding of others.

I now consider my total life experiences a blessing rather than a curse. I feel as though I have seen both sides of the coin, and now have much less trust in the "good," and much less fear of the "bad." Hardships challenge us to cope with *all* of life, and to emerge not only as survivors, but as more complete human beings.

I don't know if those who haven't been in therapy will be able to relate to what I have shared, but I think they will; life, after all, is still life. Therapy just takes life experiences and helps us integrate those experiences and put them in the proper perspective.

Jeffrey, my oldest child, graduated from high school in 1979. In 1980, Bill, my second oldest, graduated, and that same year, I received my Bachelor of Science Cum Laude. Ken graduated in 1982, Miles in 1983, and in 1985 I received my Master's Degree.

The college experience helped my self-confidence. I had a few teachers who encouraged me, especially with my writing. I felt alive and almost well at college. But then, each day, I'd return home to more physical work than I could possibly handle, and to the bleak reality of a bankrupt emotional environment. It was about this same time that our financial situation met with reversal, and for the first time in my married life I had to worry about where the money would come from to pay the bills.

In the fall of 1984 we moved to Pine City, 200 miles from our roots. We thought if we bought a less expensive farm and had a dairy operation, we could recover financially. We sold the home place in Hanska to Luther's nephew, thus keeping the farm in the family. My husband's parents were dead and my father had died also by then. Life was quickly passing by, and it often felt like it was closing in on us.

I got a job working in a group home and began taking in foster children. After two years my brother-in-law died, and my nephew moved to his father's place and no longer needed our farm. So we moved back to it, to the same little community where we'd begun; we moved back to the home place, and Luther took a job doing over-the-road trucking.

It was then, after coping for years with pain and struggles without the life-sustaining benefit of genuine intimacy, that I finally acknowledged to myself that my marriage of 29 years was a marriage in name only.

On December 10, 1988, Luther and I had a serious talk. It was the first time I'd ever mentioned the word divorce. His response was "I know you have been unhappy for a long time. Don't feel bad. We did what we wanted to do. We raised six good kids."

All I heard was, "Don't feel bad." I was crying and couldn't imagine not feeling bad about the death of a relationship. However, like a thousand times before when we had talked about something serious, we had intercourse (I wish I could say we made love). The next day was Sunday, so we went to church and to communion together. For the millionth time I asked God to forgive me.

The next day, on December 11, a Sunday afternoon, Luther left in the truck for the east coast on a long-haul delivery, carrying cheese and butter for Kraft. Less than a week later, on Friday night, December 16, he was killed instantly in a crash.

CHAPTER 7

A WORLD TORN ASUNDER

The cords of death entangled me; the torrents of destruction overwhelmed me. The cords of the grave coiled around me; the snares of death confronted me. In my distress I called to the Lord, I cried to my God for help. From his temple he heard my voice; my cry came before him, into his ears.

~ ~ Psalm 18:4-6

A simple acceptance of *all* life rather than one or the other part of it, gives a totally new conception to each act that we perform. Here lies sacredness.

~ ~ Sarah Ann Osman

How strange it is to describe chaos as a friend, but that is exactly how it has seemed these last few years. God has been good to allow the jumbled mess in my mind. For at the moment I was informed of my husband's death, it was as though my world literally fell into many and varied pieces and I hadn't a clue as to what shape it would take in the future. Just as when therapy created change in my inner life and it was like re-learning to live, now, too, I had to start all over again.

For in devastation and death there is no future or even present; only the past is a certainty. It is now the beginning of the third year following Luther's death, and there is beginning to emerge some structure out of the chaos, some form of grace and blessing that has brought me to this point. The more positive memories are what carried me along. Now that I am not so numb and my memory is more complete, now that it is beginning to allow in more of the reality, the negative along with the positive, the future is slowly beginning to seem possible once more.

Could it be that it is only as I work through my past, and sort out the mess, that the present will give me the gift of daring to dream again and believe in the possibility of tomorrow?

The world didn't stop when Luther died; it only seemed to. For these last two years I was stuck in the past, never letting myself live in the present day, and certainly not believing in tomorrow. My favorite verses; the ones that kept me going when I felt I could not go on, were:

> "Do no store up for yourselves treasures on earth, where moth and rust destroy, and where thieves break in and steal. But store up for yourselves treasures in heaven, where moth and rust do not destroy, and where thieves do not break in and steal: For where your treasure is, there will your heart be also...
>
> "Therefore, I tell you, do not worry about your life, what you will eat or drink; or about your body, what you will wear. Is not life more than food, and the body more important than clothes? Look at the birds of the air: they do not sow or reap, or store away in barns; and yet your heavenly Father feeds them. Are you not much more valuable than they?...
>
> "Seek first his kingdom and his righteousness, and all these things will be given to you as well. therefore do not worry about tomorrow, for tomorrow will worry about itself. Each day has enough trouble of its own."
>
> ~ ~ Matthew 6:19-34

Perhaps that is why it seemed almost a compulsion to spend all of my money each month. Whenever I overheard people discussing investments, retirement funds, and even savings accounts, I found myself thinking they were being totally ridiculous. The idea of a savings account seemed ludicrous. Why would I save for tomorrow? By then I might be dead, just as Luther now is dead.

First I thought if I travelled and just got away I could forget. So I spent a month in Europe, several weeks in Rio and Brazil, and I also travelled in the States. These trips were anything but enjoyable. They were torture. During better times, we would always count off the days left of a vacation, wishing we could stay longer. Now I counted backwards to see how many days before I could go home. Instead of "I can still enjoy four more days," I would think, "I only have to stay four more days."

The most amazing part of this scenario is that there was really no one to come home to, yet I wanted to go home. My children were grown and gone - and they were just as accessible by phone from any motel room as from home. So why did I need to be home? I realized that the need was not to go home, to the apartment I moved to after Luther's death, but to return home to the original farm where he and I had lived all those years, to the thirteen-room house where the memories of those years of daily living still lived on, untouched by time and death.

Each room in the old place still held a lot of memories. Perhaps someday I will have the courage to take a tour of each of those rooms and relive their stories. Maybe in the vivid remembrance of every moment of precious life that occurred in those rooms, I can lay the hopes and fears of the past to rest and thus begin to carve out a new future. Someday...

* * * * *

For now it's enough that I must, for my own healing, force myself to remember that fateful Friday night. It was just nine days before Christmas. I had taken a job in a restaurant and worked late because it was the traditional Scandinavian lutefisk supper. I had helped decorate and it went very well, but I was glad to get home. It had been a lot of work and I was tired.

Luther had called the night before to tell me that he would be gone through the weekend, working extra so that he would get home earlier on Christmas Eve. I was glad that he would be home earlier. The previous year we hadn't gone to church because he hadn't been home in time. Now my only concern was that the children and I would have to put up the Christmas tree alone, as he wouldn't be here to help. And there would not be many presents to put under it, even though I was working extra hours to help buy gifts for the children. I knew the kids were buying their father a new Bible to replace the study Bible his mother had given him a few years ago, just before she died...the one with thc worn and torn pages, that was missing most of Genesis, several pages from Psalms and Lamentations, and the front cover.

I climbed wearily up the stairs and tried to sleep. I noticed my youngest son had cleaned up the house. He wasn't home yet, and, as I fell asleep, my last thought was that I'd have to thank him tomorrow.

The next thing I knew, I heard his car in the driveway and the kitchen door open. I heard the refrigerator door and knew he was fixing himself a snack. I dozed off again. Much later, in a half sleep, I heard another car drive up. Yes, it was the door opening. I counted the kids in my mind. They were all away except the one home from college for the weekend, and by now he must be sound asleep down the hall. Perhaps it was the neighbor's son. Was tomorrow the day the boys were leaving early to go skiing? No, I was sure that was next week. In the midst of my sleep-sluggish thoughts, my son came to my room and said, "Mom, there are two men in the kitchen who want to talk to you."

How strange. I see that it is 1:10 a.m. I think, "Maybe someone ran out of gas or went into a ditch...it was a bit slippery on my way home." I have on these flimsy pajamas, so I take the time to put on a pair of slacks and a shirt. I run a comb through my hair and walk bewildered down the steps, not sure what I'm going to find.

The men have on their top coats. I think they look a bit like those people who go around evangelizing, but those people wouldn't be out this time of the night. My son stayed upstairs. I'm glad I'm not home alone. Finally the men come into more conscious focus, and I realize one of them is my husband's boss.

He says, "There's been an accident." He stops.

"Has Luther been hurt?"

"Yes."

"How bad is it?" In those milliseconds I'm thinking that he is probably in a hospital somewhere, needing me, and we don't have enough money for me to go to him.

"Real bad," he says. "The worst it could possibly be. Luther was killed."

"Oh, no! NO, NO NO!"

In his discomfort, he blurts out, "It wasn't his fault. Don't worry about money, you will be well taken care of for the rest of your life..."

"What a strange thing to say," I think. "I'm certainly not thinking about money."

* * * * *

That was two years, two months, and 25 days ago, and at that moment it was as though someone took my world, dropped it, and shattered it in 10,000 pieces.

Since then my life has been measured and calibrated by events "before the accident" and those "after the accident." In earlier years my life had been measured by which child

I was pregnant with at the time. Now the accident is the event against which all else is measured.

My eyes are wet and tears are spilling down my cheeks. At any given moment I can instantly be transported back to that black night and relive the terror. It is indelibly etched in my mind and my heart, and much of my time since then has been spent trying to "fix" the image, make it come out right this time...or simply erase it from memory if not from actuality. I try to undo that night...to bring back the world as I knew it, flawed though it was.

I would gladly exchange the two years, two months, and 25 days of my new world for just five minutes of my old, familiar world. There was so much left unfinished, things that needed to be said, that would lie forever within my heart, waiting to be spoken, waiting to find resolution or closure.

It's not that my old world was so good. I sometimes have to remind myself of that. It was actually much harder in almost every way than my life now. Aside from our emotional and marital problems, we also had more of the everyday, routine, practical problems than I have now. But they were different. They weren't so final. They had to do with bills to pay, a furnace that needed repair, maybe needing a new truck or new farm equipment. And they were familiar. They were predictable. If change occurred it happened slowly. Our life on the farm moved in slow, repetitive, predictable cycles - the cycles of nature. This was swift. This was not natural.

I think of the births of my children. A new baby changes the world of those it enters, but when I had each baby I had time to make plans, to imagine how life would change, and then I could prepare for that change. But not this time. Not this change. In one moment my life went from monotonous predictability to total chaos. Nothing, ever again, could be for sure. I lost not only a husband, I lost a world. And even though I still had my children, all of a sudden their existence also felt tenuous. They, too, could be gone in a flash.

I did not even begin to look at the pieces of my life that first year. I just clutched them tightly in my hands and heart and, like irregular pieces of clay, mashed them together and held them against this new reality which resembled nothing I'd ever seen before. It even had a new language; words like widow, wrongful death suits, attorneys, and litigation; words I'd hardly ever heard and didn't want to learn.

In the second year I began dating, but not really trusting. I didn't get serious. For quite a while I dated two men at the same time, not wanting to put all my eggs in one basket. I didn't visualize my future as anything but being alone. I reasoned that if I kept my life simple, with just myself to worry about, I would never again have another person yanked from my life and from my heart. With only myself to worry about, I felt like I had more control over the future, and therefore less to fear.

It is important for me that I not be too hard on myself for the way I have lived since the accident, because I really haven't had a choice. I had spent my life believing that we can react to life however we choose, that life deals the cards and we decide how to play them. Then, for the first time in my life, I was dealt a hand and was not able to choose how to play it, because I simply could not make sense of the cards, these fragments of my life suddenly scattered around me.

It has been a slow process, this piecing together of the shreds of a life, but it is possible; I'm doing it. Today is better than yesterday. And today there is a tomorrow.

ONCE IN MY LIFE I LOVED

For several days I've thought of you,
And cannot function well.
It seems my soul is crying out,
Fact is...it feels like hell.

There's nothing that I want to do
I only want you back.
I lie here on my couch and cry,
My whole world's drenched in black.

I know the sun will shine again
I know life will return.
It's just my heart is very sad,
And for your touch I yearn.

Then I remember I can say
Once in my life I loved.
I truly cared for someone else:
A gift from God above.

You've left me unintended gifts,
What's more, I feel I've grown.
Thanks for sharing all those years.
Now I'll learn to live alone.

THE BROKEN MIRROR

The night you died
My image broke,
The glass now lies
Upon the floor.
For years you were
My looking glass.
I looked at you
To see myself.
We became two parts
Of a whole picture.
I had only to look
Into your face or
Hear your tone of voice
And I would know
How things were going.
Until now.
Now I have no
Image of myself.
The broken pieces
Lie scattered on the floor.
Frantically,
I try to pick them up.
They no longer fit.
They hurt my hands.

I bleed. Like in a dream
I see the blood,
But I don't feel the pain.
I only know the pieces do not fit.
You are gone.
My mirror is broken.
There is no one to reflect me.
Where did I go?
When you left, "we" died.
I do not know this "me."
Like a two year old, I must
Learn to walk and talk,
And create a new world,
A world of "me,"
For the "we" lies broken
On the floor.
Jagged pieces of glass
Cut my hands,
But I must learn
To put them together again;
To separate the "you"
Pieces from the "me" pieces.
For no longer are there
Any "we" pieces...
Except in memory.

MUSINGS FROM SOUTHERN CALIFORNIA

It's been two years now since Luther died. I lie on my bed looking out to the Pacific Ocean. Palm trees line the shore, they look to be about two blocks away. I walk out onto the veranda into the 70-plus degree sunshine and feel its warmth being absorbed into my anemic soul. The sound of the air conditioner inside blocks out the sounds of the city. I step inside and turn it off.

Now I can hear as well as see the cars drift lazily by. They do not seem in any particular hurry. Perhaps they are sight seers on the way to the beach.

Was it only a little over 24 hours ago I was in Minnesota shuffling through the snow and struggling to get my suitcases to the car?

I realize as I look out that this could be Rio or Miami. All large cities look a little alike. In the resort areas the reality and ugliness of poverty are missing. They are insulated from the hardships. One does not pay to be subjected to reality. One pays to live in a fantasy where ten dollar breakfasts are the norm. Money is no longer a measure. For when one is here, it is assumed that one has travelled beyond the necessities. The luxuries have now become expected. Every room has a veranda where people sun themselves. Perhaps the natives have become so accustomed to the view that they no longer open their drapes to catch their breath at the beauty.

I begin to soak this up so I can take it back with me to the cold days just ahead; to my apartment where poverty is still a reality, luxury a fantasy, and death an everyday fact of life. The sun grows uncomfortable and I move back inside, switch on the air conditioner and retreat back into the perfectly controlled and comfortable environment.

My suitcase lies at the foot of the bed, its contents strewn about haphazardly. A partly read book, Education of a Wandering Man, lies face down, near at hand, ready to be devoured at any convenient time.

I think of the family and friends back home; home still being the old farm where I lived for so many years. I remember the dishes in the sink and wonder if my son will wash them before the food is dried on. I wonder what my friend, Fred, will think when he returns my coat - the one I wore to the airport - to the closet. What will he think of the clutter he'll encounter there. I try to believe it won't matter to him, and pretend it doesn't matter to me.

Why does the clutter matter? Is it a reflection of my life? Is my life as fragmented as the jumble of colors in my closet? I want a color coordinated life, but often the colors seem to be dictated by the demands of the moment. Each day I awake and try to organize the clutter, but it is more than I can manage...or even care to manage. Each night I promise myself that tomorrow everything will all fall into place, the colors will be in order, and the picture will be complete and whole.

Thus far that hasn't happened. I cannot even see the outline of the picture clearly, let alone the pieces or the colors, except those of my children. They are the constants, they will always be the givens. But will the rest of my life revolve only around them? No. A thousand times, no. That would not be healthy for any of us. No, I'll make a life of my own, as will they. A few friends also are forever. The juxtaposition changes, but they are my few "forever" friends.

Today I think of marriage and why marriage puts people in a separate category - a category with a shape and structure that rules out transience. By its definition marriage is exclusive and permanent. There is no longer the adventure of the unknown. In marriage one has the security of boundaries and those boundaries must be flexible, but defined.

I do not yet have my new boundaries in place. I do not have Me well enough defined to offer myself to anyone. The only gift I have to give at this time is the creature in transition.

TODAY I MISS YOU

It's Saturday, the day you'd be home.
I looked forward to that, for I'd not be alone.
At least for one night you'd sleep in our bed
And I could rest easy with nothing to dread.

Next morning we'd go to church and come home,
Make a quick meal, then you'd answer the phone:
"Yes," you'd agree to Dakota or Maine.
Each week was a new place, it was never the same.

I'd help you pack and take clothes to the car.
We'd talk on the way, though it wasn't too far.
You'd say, "There she is, all red and so clean.
Take care of the kids. You know what I mean."

"I'll be back on Friday. Pick up the check."
"Drive safely," I'd say. "Don't get in a wreck."
I'd laugh and go home, and think in my mind;
"Two weeks until Christmas - not very much time!"

Then came that night, a Friday it was,
Mitch woke me to say, "Come on down because
There's two men in the kitchen, they seem alright."
But what could they want at this time of the night?

I pulled on my pants and put on a top
Ran a comb through my hair, oh my, what a mop.
Came down to the kitchen only to find
Two men in suits, but they both seemed just fine.

A second glance and then I knew
It was your boss, he'd come about you.
Had you been hurt? Were you okay?
"No" was the word he dreaded to say.

"He's not dead?" I ask, not wanting to know.
"Yes," they said, "We're afraid it is so."
"It wasn't his fault. He hadn't a clue.
It was slippery, there wasn't a thing he could do."

Now I'm all alone on this Saturday morn.
The kids have been good, though they, too, are torn.
We know you're with God and that makes us glad,
But, oh, here on earth, we're ever so sad.

Tears help to erase a bit of the pain
But much of my life now seems lived in vain.
No one to bake cakes for, no kitchen to clean.
Who cares if it's dirty; it just won't be seen.

I miss you today much more than I say.
The hurt in my spirit prompts me to pray:
Just help me, dear God, to get through till tonight
Help me to sleep, while you make things alright.

But I know deep inside that it won't be the same.
I pretend that it will, but that's only a game.
It's Saturday morning, you're not coming home.
Today and tomorrow...I'll still be alone.

Alone and so lonely, just tears in your place,
A bed that's too big, and no smile on your face.
I treasure the memories and photos of you.
And today I'll go on...that's all I can do.

Our children are great, so loving and warm.
They try to help me each Saturday morn.
But what can they do or what can they say?
The fact is that God has taken you away.

Be waiting for me, for someday I'll come Home.
With our heavenly Father, we're never alone.
It helps me to know that our Father's the same,
And this you should know: your life wasn't in vain.

I'm happy for you, you have no bills to pay.
Life's problems are solved for you on this day.
But down here below, I want you to know,
I miss you today, and my heart's filled with woe.

Your loving wife of 29 years, Karen
January 30, 1989

FATHER

by Mitch Thormodson
(my youngest son)

I knew him as daddy,
    when I was but five,
And he helped dry my tears
    when at night I would cry.

I knew him as dad,
    as I grew to be ten,
And I started to realize
    he was not like most men.

I knew him as Father,
    as I turned eighteen
And knew he was proud,
    when for me his eye gleamed.

I knew him as friend
    when we parted that day.
And I thank God above
    I could know him that way...

Some fathers are dad,
        or daddy, or sir.
Some fathers are gone,
        just a memory or blur.

My father was friend;
        now he's gone far away.
But I know that again
        I will see him someday.

MOTHER

by Bill Thormodson
(my second oldest son)

The music is playing
The light's turned down low
The dance is beginning
She dances alone.

My mother and father were married 29 years ago. At that time, they started a dance. They danced their way through six children, and what a dance it was. They spent tens of thousands of dollars to feed them, clothe them, heal them, and make them happy. They gave their time and energy to their children. A significant part of their lives was invested in their kids. In a sense, their children were their lives.

And they loved it. They loved their children and they loved being parents. They loved feeding and caring for them, and they loved watching them grow into adults.

AND HOW THEY DANCED!

They danced through five graduations and six confirmations. They danced as five of their children became President of the local church youth group. They danced as Kenneth became a star basketball player and when Mary, Miles, or Bill played the piano. They danced when Mary or Mitch got on the honor roll and when Mary got into St. Olaf College.

And then they danced some more.

They danced when their children became involved with a temperance organization. They danced when Mary, Mitch, and Bill went on mission projects for the church. They danced when Jeff announced he would become a preacher and danced again at his wedding. And they danced when their first grandchild was born.

When father started farming again, they danced. When the new herd of cows was purchased, they danced. Over many years they danced with a multitude of friends and new faces. The dance often slowed, there were unexpected swirls and turns, but it never stopped for them. Until now.

The dancing continues
There's joy all around
"But where is my partner?"
He's not to be found.

Our parents had many dances planned. They planned on dancing at five more weddings. They looked forward to long dances with many grandchildren. This June a graduation dance was planned for Mitch. They looked forward to dancing at Jeff's ordination. Many future Christmas and Easter dances were planned with their children and family.

Now, when Miles or Mary graduates from college, who will the proud mother think of? Who had she planned to share this moment with? The man who helped mold and shape this day, that's who. And when she looks into her child's or grandchild's face, and sees her husband's features, who will she think of? Who will she want to dance with?

When Jeff is ordained, when Mary gets married...which relative will get that first dance? When Ken comes to visit and brings his family, who will Mother share her joy and pride with? Who'll dance this dance with her?

"Who'll dance with me now
That my partner is gone?"
She dances alone
But the dance still goes on.

There may be other partners to come. The dance floor is full of people. But who can replace your first partner, a partner who danced 29 years with you?

When she goes to Miles's wedding with another, can she say, "Look at our son?" When Mary gets her first real job, to whom can she say, "Look at our daughter, didn't she do well?" Who will she share her joy with? Who else could ever understand?

Another may look, act, or even talk like my dad, but no one could replace him. Though some others may come after, it will never be the same. My Mother will never again dance with her first partner, nor will she ever forget him.

The music is playing
Her partner is gone
She looks where he once was
Then dances alone.

CHAPTER 8

LETTER TO LUTHER
(Summer 1991)

Today I will visit your grave, but you are still not in it; you are still not completely dead for me. You reside somewhere between our yesterdays and my tomorrows. The other day, in a passing conversation, I overheard someone say, "He never let his wife die." It occurred to me that I haven't let you die either. For these past two and a half years I have kept you alive. Was it to punish myself? As if my suffering would bring you back perhaps? I did not believe it fair for me to continue to live and be happy without you, when you would never again have your own happy days. Slowly, slowly I am beginning to let you die, to let you go. Not your memory - that will die only with my last breath - but you.

It's the memories that keep you alive, and yet I know it's the memories that will eventually allow me to let you go. In my mind I continually relive our life together, putting all the pieces together into a new shape I can now live with, a shape I can understand. To do that, I often revisit the old home place, the family farm.

There I need only walk in the front door and I am hit with powerful memories and emotions. On my last visit there, up in the attic, I found your cap, the one you wore on your last trucking trip. As I held it in my hands and felt the soft material that had encircled your head, once again I dissolved into tears.

An image comes to my mind of one of those peddlers of the Old West who would drive through the countryside peddling his wares. His sales were not dependent on what people needed, but on what brought back memories for them. The people he approached would say things like, "We used to have one of these when I was just a tyke," and they would promptly buy it, whatever it was. Memories are seductive. They sometimes take you places you don't want to be, but, in compensation, the good ones can never be taken from you.

Remember when Jeffrey became deathly ill when he was only eight months old? His fever was 105 when we took him to the Madelia Hospital, and then they had us take him to Mankato hospital. I remember the doctor going by and saying, "This is what gives parents gray hairs." I prayed, "Dear God, I love this little boy so much. Thank you for letting him live with us these eight months. I cannot imagine life without him, yet I know he is yours and you can take him back. You have only loaned him to us. If it be Thy will, please let him stay." I went home sadly that night knowing that God could indeed take him and I had no assurance He would not. However, Jeffrey healed overnight, and we took him home three days later.

How we rejoiced the day we brought him home again. We didn't know then that that was the first of many crises in our life together. Remember when he was 16 and we got a call in the middle of the night? "Mom, can you pray?" I said I was sure I could, but what should I pray about? He said, "I was going out to get milk and Brian and I just spun around in the car and hit a telephone pole. We're at Mr. Moe's house. He said he'll bring us home. But pray Daddy won't be mad." Of course you weren't angry, just thankful he was okay.

Then there was the day he came home and said he was joining the Air Force. I turned to you and said, "What shall we do?" You, in your quiet and certain wisdom, said, "Let him go." Not long after that, he called and said he and his girlfriend Jeanne were coming to visit, and at the end of the visit he said they were getting married. Jeff was

19, Jeanne 18. As much as I didn't want them marrying that young, I'm glad now they did, so that we had a chance to share the wedding of at least one of our children, as well as the later birth of a grandchild.

It was experiences like these that cemented our marriage. The crises we lived through together and the love we had for our children formed the basis of our relationship.

Jeffrey has been on my mind today, for tomorrow he will graduate from college and go on to the seminary. I want you to be there with me; I don't want to go alone. I want you to walk with me and squeeze my hand when his name is announced and he walks across the stage. I don't want you dead and I don't want you in heaven. I want you here to hold your granddaughter during the ceremony, as I know you would, and later bring her home with us for a while so Jeanne and Jeff can have some time alone together.

It's these special days like Jeff's graduation that leave me feeling so powerless; powerless to bring you back, powerless to make things be the way they would have been. I want to undo your death, but can't. No matter how much I cry and no matter how much I pray, you won't be here tomorrow. Instead, today I will go to the cemetery and put flowers on your grave and try once again to let you die so I can live.

* * * * * *

In my search for myself I have discovered that the reason I felt so guilty and remorseful is because I was thinking of leaving you, and then, in a strange twist of fate, you left me.

In my mind I wanted to make the picture perfect, even in my grief. I wanted to see us as the perfect loving couple, eagerly raising our six children in a garden of happiness. I now know that to force that picture would hurt my soul, for it's not true. That's not the way it was. The truth is it wasn't even close to that; I had never been more miserable. In fact, I had despaired of ever being happy. I had decided I had two choices in life: To continue in a marriage that had long since been lacking in real intimacy, or to leave the marriage and hope to be able to some day begin again with someone new. I hadn't yet firmly decided which course to follow, I only knew something vital was missing, I was unhappy, and I felt like a failure.

After the move from Hanska to Pine City where we believed we could start over, we moved back to Hanska after only two years. We had left the old home place, but we had also taken our troubles with us, only to eventually bring them all back with us to Hanska. Once back on the farm, you took the job driving a truck, for a week at a time, leaving me with a house that was sadly in need of repair, a furnace that didn't heat the house, bills that I could see no hope of ever getting paid, and endless frustrations. With you on the road, all the kids called home needing guidance and assistance, and I was the only one there to the carry the load. I couldn't cope and I felt I should have been be able to.

Then you died. They said that ten seconds after the truck hit you, you were dead. I begged them to tell me a lie. I wanted desperately to hang on to you. I did not want the truth, but I remember the look on your boss's face and the cry that came from my mouth. I screamed like a mad woman. I wanted to hit my head against the wall and scream from the unbearable pain inside. "NO, NO, NO," I screamed. I called the boys downstairs and told them the news. They stood wide-eyed for an eternity of seconds, then burst into tears and slowly found their way back upstairs. I called my brother and the pastor to come stay with me for a while. After they were gone I lay on the couch alone and waited for Jeff and Mary to come. It was the longest night of my life.

My body and spirit were numb. It would be days before the reality would hit and months before I could function at any level except minimally. I remember how I would be driving and suddenly not know where I was going, and I was forever forgetting where I'd left my car in parking lots.

Shortly after your death, when I went with a real estate man to look at homes, all the times you and I looked for a farm came rushing back. That old house, so badly in need of repair, now felt like a wonderfully warm place, a place I wanted to return to. I didn't want to look at newer and nicer homes. I didn't want to make any decisions. I wanted to say, "Whatever you think" - but no one was there. Maybe I didn't think I deserved a nice home. I seemed to continue to believe I needed to be punished for telling you I was thinking of divorce.

When you died I felt like you deserted me in mid-stream; you became an unfinished sentence hanging forever in the air. I wanted to scream, "Come back and finish this part of our lives and then you can leave!" If our marriage had been going well, maybe moving on might have been less painful. I believe it is much easier to move into a new life if the one you left was happy and peaceful. I have come to believe that when a person dies and the one left behind feels there was unfinished business, it is much more difficult to move on with life.

* * * * * *

I wonder whatever happened to your underwear and socks. I know the boys took your shirts and sweaters; even today they each have a favorite sweater of yours. I have the one I gave you that last birthday. But I still don't remember what happened to your underwear. Strange, what things surface after all this time. And I still can't remember what I wore to your funeral. I have no idea. I remember what I wore to my father's funeral and to your mother's funeral - but I have no recollection of what I wore to your funeral. Me, who was always so conscientious about how I looked. Somehow that was totally unimportant the day of the funeral. Funny how death strips away all facades and leaves only the stark, cold fact: You are dead and I am alone.

* * * * * *

Nights have gotten a little better, but tonight I feel like I just need a safe harbor from the storm and someone to hold me in their arms. Just let me pretend that you are still here, that life is still safe, and that there's nothing to fear. Tears form in my eyes and my throat fills with pain. I don't think I can go on any longer. Everything seems so futile. Who cares what day it is, or what the weather's like, or if the house is cleaned.

There was a time - was it just a few years ago? - that I had two jobs, a house full of children, and no time to rest. Now I have nothing but time. Endless hours of heartache and uncertainty. Grief moves in such unpredictable waves. One day I think I'm ready to move on with my life, the next day I'm full of fear and doubt.

* * * * * *

There's something unforgettable about realizing for the first time that you are on your own. No one is there to help clean the house for company, lock all the doors at bedtime, or fix the septic tank when it backs up in the basement. When our septic tank backed up, I couldn't even find the darned thing. We ended up digging up the whole lawn trying to find it because I kept thinking I knew where it was, but was wrong.

I think it was then that I finally and fully allowed myself to hate you for dying. I felt deserted and angry. Why would I know where the septic tank was? You had always taken care of these things and now you weren't here when I needed you. How dare you leave me without telling me all I needed to know to live!

After many bitter tears and a gut-wrenching rage, I was then able to review some of the more positive aspects of our relationship, and see them in a new light. I recalled with regret the times I just wanted to be alone to write without having to worry about being interrupted, never realizing at the time the many things you did to make this possible. You did so many things to make my life run smoother for me, and I never fully appreciated them at the time.

Just your presence in the room let me relax. When you were home I could do my own thing and not worry about the children. When you were on the road trucking, I had the full responsibility for the house and children, but I could always call your boss to find out how to reach you, and I'd always know within a few days when you'd be home again to help lighten my load. Now you are never coming home again. I am on my own and that's a lonely place to be.

* * * * * * *

Now that four of the children are married, I have come to see that we cannot always judge the significance of our lives. While you were alive, I never realized the immense impact you were having on the children because I was too close to the situation. Now in death, with the distance, the values you passed on to them have crystallized; they have taken the best you gave and incorporated it into their lives.

When our first grandson was born to Mary Kay, our only daughter, he was named Joshua Luther. In that tiny little fellow I saw the resemblance to his mother and also to you. Even though you are dead, a part of you lives on through our grandchildren. I feel how proud you would have been, and tears slip down my cheeks, as I wish this new little person could walk with you in the fields and listen to you read him stories as you did with our children. But I know that is never to be. You will be a part of his life only through pictures of you, and pictures are so lifeless and silent. One moment of life is worth 10,000 pictures and yet, when a picture is all we have, it becomes precious.

* * * * * *

The gift you have given me in death is the knowledge that I am dispensable. Your death has put life into a new perspective. For twenty years I had wanted to write a book, but always put it off thinking there was time for that after I retired. With your death I realized "if it was going to be, it was up to me." I now know life does not come with tomorrow guaranteed. It is only today we are promised. I was aware that all my good intentions and boxes full of notes would be burned with my death unless I did something today.

Now that I know I am dispensable, our children seem to find me almost indispensable. Perhaps this has to do with my returning ability to move out of myself and think once again of others.

It is important to grieve and mourn, and there is a time for self-centeredness in the healing process. But there is also a time for moving out, and rather than waiting and asking what others can do for us, we must be looking around for those we can help. I have just returned this morning from nine days away from home. I met some wonderful new people and realized that all over this earth there are interesting, caring people who have hurting hearts just as I do, but even if it's for only a few moments in passing, we can share with each other and enrich each other's lives.

Now, finally, I see that God has reached into my heart and begun to help me make sense of my life and myself again. The tools I gained from therapy, along with God's grace, have helped me to move on, and in that moving on I have seen more clearly myself, you, and our relationship.

SINCE YOU'VE GONE

I've learned to value each moment,
I've learned to sing a new song,
I'm learning to be much more patient,
And not say, "It's taking too long."

I'm learning to fill in the spaces
With tasks that I know I must do.
I do them now gladly for others,
Without my depending on you.

Thank you for giving me memories.
Thank you for giving me life.
Thank you for blessed assurance
And for holding my hand in the strife.

The seasons of Life now are changing.
As over Life's pathways I trod,
And if this be my springtime or winter,
I leave that decision to God.

DYING

The spirit is a fragile marvel wrapped tenderly inside each of us. The body, like a flower's petals, hides within it the secret seed. If one is to see behind the petals to the soul, one must put off haste and harshness, for dissonant voices and lack of reverence for the process shatter flower and soul alike.

As flowers mature and die, they shed their colors slowly and only knowing eyes perceive the purpling of the rose. There is a great consolation when the blue at last shows through: It will then not be long before all petals fall and leave revealed, within our view, the eternal soul - the most beautiful vision of all.

Often those too busy with daily living take no time to heed the dying side within. But how essential for completion and contentment that, as the petals begin to fall, we honor the beauty of their presence and of their passing. For it is in their transience that we are allowed to view fully the glory of the core and to reaffirm a life well lived.

CHANGE

Morning comes,
the sun shines, and
I know this minute
brings an end to dreams.
It is in the letting go
that one finds strength
to have no expectations,
to need no great words of wisdom,
only silence - moving
gracefully across the hills
as the sun finally sinks
in the West. It is enough
to have known love once.
It is enough.

CHAPTER 9

ORDER AND GRACE OUT OF CHAOS

Called or not called, God is always there.

~ ~ Carl Jung

It is in knowledge as in swimming; he who flounders and splashes on the surface makes more noise and attracts more attention than the pearl diver who quietly dives in quest of treasures to the bottom.

~ ~ Washington Irving

When death hit the core of my being, I was forced to reevaluate my own life. Reality reigns. People die. It doesn't matter how healthy I am, or how young, I can still die in an instant. One minute I can be here and the next dead. So I'd better be doing what fulfills me and gives my life meaning and not waste whatever time remains.

I am 53 years old and I believe the best years of my life are just ahead. I do not believe I am on a downhill slide to the grave. Each phase of my life has brought special kinds of joy, and I am always listening to myself and trying to see what I can learn from each struggle or joy I go through. That insures that I will keep on growing as a person.

When Luther died I could have remained in a hopeless state; like a bud that comes on the rose bush too close to the killing frost and dies on the vine. In my working with widows and widowers I saw some people who felt that the best was over for them and they were just waiting to die. Inside they had already died with the spouse.

Another kind of person I have seen is the one who just feels stuck. Unless they become unstuck, they will never bloom and become the person they could have been. Excuses rule their lives. They are too poor, their kids don't mind them, their friends don't support them, their marriages are bad, their bosses don't appreciate them; the list is endless.

We all feel powerless at times, and during those times we become vulnerable to our own negative messages. But if we continue to disparage and berate ourselves, we become not only emotionally weakened, but physically weakened as well. Illness and disease take advantage of this weakened state. If, on the other hand, we can be compassionate with ourselves while simultaneously acknowledging our deepest pains, healing can occur and we will once again be able to face the world with a glad heart.

I've noticed that we expect people to say they're fine when asked. If they begin to share their concerns, we are uncomfortable and hurry to get away, leaving them to their despair. Only in crisis are we encouraged to cry and show our emotions; otherwise we are supposed to grin and bear it. If we want to help people to heal from within, we need to learn to accept them for what and where they are emotionally, without any judging, shaming, questioning, or expectations.

I now see life as both an inward and an outward journey with many deaths and resurrections along the way. The rose bush is not always blooming, and to the casual observer, I may be doing the most when it appears I'm doing the least. The days like today, when I never leave the house and I spend the day in my basement room with nothing more than my pen and paper, are the days I long for and cherish. These are the days when I grow.

Today I understand better why, over 20 years ago, I wanted to be around my therapist as much as possible. He was like water when my soul was dying of thirst. I believe that if I had not started therapy I would have been dead by the age of forty; I was that unhappy. I now see that therapy, in effect, is self-healing and an on-going process. Even though I no longer see a therapist, I continue to look inside myself. With all the stresses of life and the needs of others, it's easy to ignore or lose touch with that deeper self. But I can't grow from within, and I can't let God's love flow freely through me, if I don't pay attention to what my own soul needs.

I have always enjoyed writing and found that my journals and notebooks have been my greatest tools in uncovering my inner self. In looking back at my journals from years before beginning therapy, I've found that there were glimpses of truth in my writing, even then, that I was unable to detect or learn from at the time. Often I didn't understand the things I wrote when I wrote them, but they felt true, they felt right at the moment. Still today, my inner truth is elusive. It is possible to grasp only when I acknowledge that I need time to be alone with myself, to be still and to reflect on the ageless truth, "Be still and know that I am God" (Psalms 46:10), and to come to know God within me.

I found that another of the things I need is conversation with others on a deep level. With those friends who have helped me grow, we rarely talk about the weather, world news, home decorating, or sick kids. We talk about feelings and wonder and joy and pain and things that matter to the soul. We talk about our perceptions of God.

I have one friend, Madlyn, who has helped me tremendously. Our children are about the same age and, two years before Luther was killed, her oldest daughter was killed in an auto accident. For over 30 years we have met almost every week for lunch and to talk about our lives. When Luther died, she was the first person I wanted by my side.

Another friend, Chris, has helped me undo some of the religious shame and misperceptions of my early years. Chris is a very unorthodox woman who does not consider herself a Christian. Yet since she, too, is searching for her inner light, she considers herself spiritual. She and I have shared many insights and I love her deeply. I also have a new friend of just one year who is another fellow searcher.

She is a non-traditional mother of four, an author, and is in the seminary. She and I share many insights. Even though sometimes we outgrow our friends as our interests change, this is not always the case. Sometimes friendships, like these, have lasting bonds that promote healing and are good for the soul.

Today I believe in a loving God who lives inside of me, and if I follow what is right, He is pleased. I believe He helps me all the time, in all areas of my life. I do not have a blueprint for life anymore, but each day is an adventure as I try to listen to God more closely, through His words, and do what is right for me at every moment. My life is unfolding. It is enough to trust that there is a plan for my life. Today I hope and expect to live the rest of a long life in touch with both the bright and dark sides of existence. I try to share the light whenever I feel it, and I try to ease the darkness of others when I can.

I once believed I could do anything I set my mind to. Now that no longer seems true or important. Each day is a new beginning, each night a restful ending. I do not make such long term plans anymore. I roll with the punches more easily now. Accomplishments seem less important, and quiet time alone has become my most cherished goal and friend. Contemplation now brings fulfillment.

* * * * *

Contemplation, while ultimately bringing fulfillment, is not always easy, however. I wonder if there is a parent alive who can look back on their years of parenting without some regrets. As I let my mind wander through my heart, I sometimes have memories of when the children were little, memories that hurt. With my third son Kenny, for example, I was so sick and so tired much of the time when he was little. I'm sure I put him in his crib for a nap when he wasn't tired, and I probably spanked him when he didn't deserve to be spanked.

Today Kenny and I are very close in a different way than I am with the others. His friends were always very important to him and he had many more friends than any of his siblings. He is still using his ability to connect with people as a professional photographer. We work together now; Kenny takes the pictures and I sell them to the families.

He also owns a fishing tackle manufacturing company and a resort. Our entire family enjoys going to Kenny's resort on Deer Lake, and some of the lakes we fish are the same ones where I used to fish with my father. Kenny is providing us a place to make new memories, and I treasure that. I am very proud of Kenny and I'm sure he has forgiven me for the times I couldn't always listen to his needs when he was little. Yet that is one of my regrets.

Another painful memory has to do with my oldest son, Jeffrey. When he was only five years old he helped me with the other three children. I didn't realize how much I expected of him until years later when he was away at Bible camp. I was cleaning his room and found a letter he'd written to his girlfriend, now his wife, Jeanne. They had been discussing child-rearing, and Jeffrey said if he was ever to have children he would raise them just as he had been raised. Then he went on to say, "However, this is very hard because I've always felt so responsible that I knew the consequences of my behavior were entirely mine. I grew up so fast I really didn't have time to be a child."

I realized then that I had expected an awful lot from him. When he returned from camp I told him how sorry I was. I said I'd try to take care of the younger kids myself and not expect him to drive them around so much or take responsibility for them. I said I'd give him more time for himself. We cried together and I tried to keep my part of the bargain, but I knew the past could not be redone.

When he was 18 years old, Jeffrey joined the Air Force and then married Jeanne at 19. They have been married 14 years and have a darling five year old girl, Denae, the only grandchild Luther ever met. Jeffrey is now in seminary preparing to be a pastor. I'm glad his father knew he had chosen that profession before he died. He was always close to Jeffrey and very proud of him. Jeffrey is the most like his father in his mannerisms. Even though I have some regrets, I feel we must have done something right, as all of our children have become wonderful adults:

Jeffrey is in his third year at the seminary and next year will be an ordained Missouri Synod Lutheran pastor. He and Jeanne and Denae live in St. Louis.

Bill, our second son is completely restoring the old 13-room family farmhouse where Luther and I lived, making it into a Bed and Breakfast. He and Debbie have a daughter, Olivia, who is 18 months old, and a son, Peter Joseph, born June 18, 1993.

Kenneth, as I mentioned earlier, is a professional photographer.

Miles, an automation engineer, and his wife, Susan, live in Portage, Wisconsin. Their daughter, Arielle, will be a year old October 24, 1993. She was born on my father's birthday, the one for whom her father, Miles, was named. She's her parents' joy and delight.

Mary was married February 29, 1992 and Joshua Luther was born March 19, 1993 to her and her husband, Dale. She is a full-time mother and volunteers as an advocate for battered women. Mary and Dale plan someday to be missionaries.

Mitch, my youngest son, is a missionary with Youth With a Mission. He is in Russia and plans to remain for several years. I miss Mitch a lot. Since he was still home when Luther died, he lived with me during those first few months and grieving together drew us especially close.

* * * * *

There is a small lake on the old home place property called Linden Lake. Luther and his mom had gone there when he was a child, and when he and I were first married, we used to take a flashlight and I would fish in the dark after all the chores were done. More than once, after the babies were born, we'd drive down to the lake and he'd stay in the car with the little ones while I'd fish.

That lake had a wonderful therapeutic value for our family. When I was upset, I'd walk to the lake to sort out my thoughts. When the kids were upset they'd storm out of the house and head for the lake. In a few hours they'd be back and we could talk peacefully. Sometimes the kids would walk or ride the tractor along the lake road with their daddy at sunset and talk about their day. It was a natural healing place where each of us went to escape the harshness of the world, and where we gained the strength to then return to it.

Raising our children was a great challenge, yet a beautiful experience. Each is now a delightful, caring human being and we all have good relationships with each other. While my regrets are painful, they are few, and I feel blessed with the outcome. I still enjoy driving the tractor and taking my children, and now my grandchildren, along the road to Linden Lake for a talk, or to take them fishing, just as we have always done down on the farm.

* * * * * *

This book helped me to integrate my experiences. Much of my life I had thought that the goal was to have as many "good" days as possible and forget the painful ones. Avoiding pain and making good memories had been my goal.

I had an uneasy awareness that something in that philosophy was not quite right, but I was never able to put my finger on the problem until one day when I was working in my garden...

I was enjoying my lilac bush in full bloom when I remembered how few blossoms it had the previous year and I wondered why. Then I recalled that I had pruned it severely during the fall. I wondered at the time if it would even survive because I had pruned it so much, and now it was far more beautiful than it had ever been. I asked myself, "Is that how Life treats us, too?"

In John 15:1-5, when Jesus refers to himself as the vine and the disciples as the branches, he tells them that if they are to bear more fruit, they must be pruned. But pruning is painful and pain is something I had always wanted to avoid. Now I could see how necessary it is to prune, to endure the pain, to rid the spirit of old and useless things, to allow for new growth.

Death of a loved one is a great pruning device. Death helps us to put life into perspective. The passing of a generation, especially, is a painful milestone. I remember how much it affected our lives when Luther's parents died. It takes a few years following that kind of loss to again find a reason for living. However, I have found that the greatest blessings have come to me as I have been able to see the painful parts of my life, not as punishment, but as pruning. I now have the faith that nothing will happen in this life that will not be the path to bearing more fruit.

I am thankful for all of my life. It has been the hardships as well as the happiness that has given me the energy to face the future with expectation. The best years of my life are yet to be, for my capacity for fruit-bearing increases with each new sorrow, with each new day. Having been a florist for several years, I am reminded that the perfume of the flower is most poignant and beautiful as the flower nears death. Would that my life, too, end with a profusion of fruit and fragrance.

CHAPTER 10

REGENERATION OF LOVE

Heaven arms with love those it would not see destroyed.

~ ~ Lao Tze

Where there is no love, there is also no truth.

~ ~ Ludwig Feuerbach

It was just a simple thing, just an oversight. One too many places set, counted wrong. Yet it seemed more than an accident that on one side of me was the man I intended to marry and, on the other side, a plate and an empty chair.

Even though I no longer lived there, it was the old home place. Our son and daughter-in-law lived there now and had invited me and my new fiance, Fred, to dinner for Mother's Day. And I had set the table, inadvertently also setting a place for Luther. The kids made jokes about the extra place, and I got up and removed the china as quickly as I could, then moved over to fill up the empty space.

But that empty space was still there in all our hearts, especially on holidays. Holidays presented a challenge, along with any special occasion days, and even Sundays because Sundays were times of family togetherness.

My children didn't want me to marry again, that's just a fact. Change is difficult for everyone. It was hard for the children to see me as an individual, for they, too, still saw the "we" of Luther and me.

Mary, especially, did not want me to re-marry. She wanted her dad back again. She, too, was about to marry and she wanted her dad back to walk her down that longest aisle of all. She wanted to tell him of her prince and her life plans. She didn't need him to talk, but to listen in silence as she knew he always did so well. But since he was not there, she shared her joys with me, and I, perhaps thoughtlessly, told her of my new love. This she did not want to hear.

She was inwardly angry that I could be happy without Luther here. She wanted me to share her happiness and not impose mine. We both were in transition and, without Luther's kindness and patience, without the familiar, it was difficult.

I just wanted to have a place to call home again, a safe place where the children could come and where I could be their mom again.

There had been too many goodbyes and too few hellos in my life. Luther died, the children graduated, left for college, married - all moving on with their lives. I was no longer the center of their attention. They had assumed I could take care of myself now and that life would go on for me without them. Yet they, too, resisted life going on without their dad. They resisted their mother starting a new life.

I knew well from previous times in my life how to avoid pain. But in avoiding pain I would also avoid pleasure, and I wasn't going to do that again. I knew I couldn't have one without the other, but right then it felt like the pain weighed too much and the pleasure was too scary. Just when I thought everything might be alright again, that I was past the worst of the pain, I crumbled and choked on my tears again.

Perhaps my beginning to open up and love again was leaving me vulnerable, for I found that I felt out of control quite often those days. I wondered if the loneliness of reality was better than a fantasy of closeness. Could I really ever allow myself to be close again? I might marry another, but there would always be that spot in my heart where Luther is loved, and, in those moments when time is suspended, I would always remember and be sad.

And yet Fred has now become woven into the fabric of my life, and there is beginning to be a new "we." My trust in God has allowed me to experience once again that I am still capable of loving. My broken heart, while not yet fully mended, is healing through God's presence. His promise of light and hope leads me on, no matter how hard I, in my fear, seem to resist.

It occurs to me that security is an illusion, one that we seem to need in order to relax and enjoy life. The illusion that a piece of paper called a marriage license will hold lasting peace and the end of worries is just that...an illusion. One is never ready for change, but change is a part of life. Change must be accepted and embraced instead of being wrestled with. I must not only submit, but I must embrace change. My fear is creating my discomfort, my pain, and my resistance. I am afraid to let go because of my fear of the unknown. As if I ever have the known. As if I ever, even for a minute, am able to control the future. Who do I think I am? Do I imagine I am God and know what the future holds just because of the past?

This change, this turmoil in my life, need not be the end, but a new beginning. My whole life stretches before me like a canvas, and I can choose not only the colors but the designs I will make. Stretching one's limits and accepting new things is never comfortable. It's quite scary.

The biggest truth of death is the disorientation and the jumping back and forth between memories and hope for a future life. There is no continuous line of thoughts or feelings, like army ants marching in order. Grief is, as always, fragmented, ragged, raw, and confusing. One moment's certainty is another moment's doubt.

I am still awed at times at the many facets of grief. Sometimes I feel almost like I am invisible and just watching life instead of living it. When all the conversation was going on at dinner that day, it was like I was a stranger standing in the wings. I wanted everyone to talk to each other and leave me out of it, because for the first time in my life, I didn't know what to say. I didn't want to have to talk, not even to those to whom I was closest.

And no one ever told me about the lethargy of grief. Sometimes I seem immobilized, like I can't move. I dread the slightest effort. Sometimes nothing seems to matter. Those times scare me. What if I remarry and have all this work to do and can't make myself move. Will Fred understand? Has he, too, labored under this heavy and jumbled load? Will he know what it is like to have a life too muddled to sort out, with no end in sight, so it's better not to start anything? It is easy to understand how the lonely become disorganized and untidy. When we suffer a loss, so much energy is focused inward, trying to make sense of the new shape of our world, that there's nothing left for the simple routines of life. I forget to make my bed or wash the dishes. I even forget to pay the bills. Friends say, "Call me sometimes," but I never do. Everything simple becomes a major chore, and anything major becomes impossible.

Meanwhile, where is God? I think the most difficult part for me to understand had not as much to do with God as with me. The very verse that I quoted so often to others,

Romans 8:28, now seems most difficult: "All things work together for good for those who love God." I know that Luther was a good man and we both loved God. Even though we were having difficult times in our marriage at the time of his death, that certainly did not seem like a fair resolution. Somewhere in my life I had been taught that life is fair. I no longer believe that. Good and bad things happen to all of us for no logical reasons, but that's a hard fact to accept.

Initially, after the accident, I thought I'd never want to marry again. The first man I dated seriously was almost exactly as Luther had been - incapable of genuine, sustained intimacy. My emotional life became a roller coaster when I was with him. One day he was warm and loving, the next day he was cool and distant. My children liked him and that was my first clue that he was their father all over again. I think if I had married him it would have been to punish myself for Luther's death. Because of the wrongful death suit and the fact that I had gotten some money, I felt guilty. I also felt guilty because Luther had died and not me, and, because of all the guilt, I could have made a huge mistake. I might have married just anyone, thereby allowing myself to be - actually ensuring that I would be - miserable again.

When I started dating an emotionally healthy person who liked himself, life, and me, I thought at first he must be acting. I was sure it would wear off when he got to know me better and I him. I was totally paranoid, and it was only after 18 months that I decided Fred was for real. He did love me for me and not for what I could do for him. He loved me whether I cleaned the house or not. He loved me in the morning as much as he had the night before. And he missed me when we were apart. I began to have the first truly healthy relationship of my life.

Before meeting Fred, when I went out on a date I was the happiest when the evening was over and I was alone again. Then I met Fred and, when I was with him, I breathed easier. I always hated that we had to part, and I still do. Just being in the same room with him enlivens me; I feel whole, complete, and at ease. I love working with him, and it makes me so happy every time he comes in a room, says "hi," and hugs me.

Before I met Fred I had had a lot of insights and warmth and caring inside, but without anyone to share with, I was lonely and frustrated. I listened to "how to" tapes and read "how to" books, and they reinforced all I believed to be true, but it still seemed as though no one really understood my plight. I am not comfortable discussing the weather, or the latest news or sports story for very long. I also can read only so many books and listen to so many tapes before I want another human being with whom I can share my insights, experiences, and my true inner being. Finding such a person was not easy.

It's not so much that people don't care anymore, as it is that the art of listening and sharing from the gut level has been lost. People in today's society are so involved in making money, watching television, or being "busy" that genuine, sincere, heart-felt dialogue is becoming extinct.

Before, my life had dimensions, but I too was so busy trying to fill the holes I felt within, that I missed what life was all about. I used to always be going someplace, doing something. I hated staying home. Now that I have someone to truly share with, someone who listens and loves with all his heart, I am eager to stay home.

In my first marriage, when Luther was home, I wanted to be gone. That is still very hard for me to admit, but it's true. Luther did not really accept me, therefore we could never connect, never feel totally comfortable with each other. I felt I was never "right" for him the way I was; I wasn't enough like his mother. During the first years of marriage I pretended to be, but, because I was pretending, the real me was never acknowledge or accepted. After therapy, when I let my real self emerge, I never felt that Luther liked me.

Of course before therapy, *I* didn't like me. I was a plastic person. I was like a chameleon; I changed to suit the environment. If you asked me how I felt, I'd wonder how you wanted me to feel. Then I'd try to feel that way no matter what my inside was saying or who I really was.

Having found a man who is capable of opening up, of talking about what is going on, and of loving me exactly as I am, has greatly improved the quality of my life. The surest way to help people change is to love them exactly as they are.

Once while Fred and I were dating, he told me how, when I had been off working in Wisconsin and he was out in the fields seeding his wheat, he found himself torn emotionally. Even though he usually enjoyed planting, he was torn because he wanted so much to be with me, or at least to have me in the house where he would be able to be with me in a few hours. What a delight it was to have someone say and mean those words, and to feel the same in return.

Having met and decided to marry Fred, I realized just how afraid I had been of this new adventure. I had carried so much pain inside for so many years that until I found a means of releasing that pain and putting into perspective my own feelings, there had been no chance of moving on with my life. Finally, the realization that I did not have to forget the past in order to have a future, filled me. I was now grateful for my whole life, for, through all of the experiences, I had grown and gained strength. Pain and pleasure are two sides of the same coin. Just as sunshine and rain are both equally necessary for the plants to grow and for rainbows to appear, so, too, are pain and pleasure necessary for human beings to flourish and mature.

EPILOGUE

And so we married. Fred is now my husband and my best friend, and we are happily working together to create a new life for both of us. Fred has the openness and life experiences to be able to identify with my struggles, so I no longer feel alone. I feel total support, both from him and for him, and I relish this new existence.

Fred's first marriage ended in a very painful divorce which he did not want, so I am learning a lot about the effect that has on children. Fred is ten years younger than I, and his youngest children are eight year old twins. This has not been an easy adjustment for me since all my children are grown. In addition, he has three other children, ages 10, 11, and 16. I believe the struggles we have regarding how much time the children should visit our home, and trying to figure out how much time Fred and I need alone together are our greatest challenges right now.

In my head I know how important the time spent with his children is to him and to them, so I feel some guilt when I say we need time alone without the children. But in my heart I know that for our marriage to remain strong, we must make the time to be alone with no distractions. Relationships, like gardens, require time and attention, nurturing and cultivating. Looking back I can see that in my first marriage I spent all my energy on the children, and little on Luther, and the marriage suffered for it.

I know that with persistence, and being able to talk to each other about our dreams and our frustrations, we will eventually reach satisfactory solutions, no matter what the problem. To have a solid marriage, I also believe it is important to have it centered on core principles held by both partners, rather than it being self- or other-centered.

Now that I have a relationship that is nourishing my total being, I understand the word intimacy much better. It is not one person feeding off the other, but mutual nourishing. I used to believe that "if you haven't got it within, there is nowhere else to go for it." I no longer believe it is quite that simple. We can gain a lot from others, as well as give to them; the exchange itself builds strength and opportunity for renewal.

Genuine love increases over time. I love Fred more now than when we first met and that love seems to grow stronger day by day. For the first time in my life I am beginning to understand how, after 25 years of marriage, it will be possible to be more in love with him than I was the day we married. Most of my life I saw marriage as a restriction to growth. I now see marriage as a wonderful place in which to grow and blossom, both individually and together.

The painful parts of my past have now become stepping stones to my future. So many things I once saw as barriers now seem like old friends, urging me on. I never imagined life could be so good and each new day could hold so much promise. I'm excited to get up each morning, although I love the nighttime equally, for that is when Fred and I talk and are just together, sharing and exchanging the energy of intimacy.

When Fred is gone I'm perfectly content knowing he will return and will be just as happy to see me as I am to see him. I never imagined one person could make such an immense difference in my life. I once loved to be around people; the more the better. Now that I find such emotional fulfillment with my husband, I am much more apt to be by myself or possibly with one or two special friends. Crowds no longer hold the appeal they once did. My happiness comes now more from the peace within than with anything external.

When I began my journey toward inner wholeness I was very fragmented. I was going in ten directions at the same time and could not focus for long on any one of them. This last year has been the first time in my life that I actually enjoyed hours and hours of uninterrupted writing. I think this new ability to center myself has to do with the return of stability to my life. The structure I now have is due in large part to the solid relationship I have with Fred.

Another beneficial result of the therapy process is the healing of the memories that occurs. However, this does not happen automatically. Recalling the painful parts of my childhood, and reliving the grief following Luther's death, brought back the pain and allowed the old wounds to be re-examined. To my surprise, it also feels like each fresh re-examination promotes deeper healing.

Because of my own healing I have been able to forgive my mother and we are now friends. Now I know in my heart that she raised us the best way she knew how. Forgiveness, empathy, and peace of mind are the rewards for remembering and reliving the pain. It occurs to me that, like a sore that festers without healing air, so is the wound of forgotten memories without exposure to the healing light of the conscious mind.

If my first marriage had been better, I would not be able to appreciate the differences in this marriage. If I had not experienced the death of a spouse, I would not now be able to identify with those who grieve. If my childhood had been ideal, I would not be able to understand dysfunctional families. If I had never been sick, I could not appreciate how well I am most of the time. These are just a few of the many blessings I now count in my life.

* * * * * *

Today I am looking outside and the window is covered with lovely patterns of Minnesota frost. The calendar says it is spring, but the wind is howling and it is snowing. It has been four years since Luther's death and, looking back, I recognize many patterns in both our relationship and in myself. These patterns, like the frost on the window, feel etched into my existence, and yet, like the frost, are impermanent and vulnerable to warmth. I have become a different person. I no longer feel driven and frozen as I once did. There is now a comfort in the wind and snow because I know that, perhaps as soon as tomorrow, the frost will melt and be replaced by signs of spring.

Life no longer has a destination. The journey itself is now the goal, and each day a new beginning. Just a few days ago I saw a robin. I hope he, too, has found shelter from the storm.